MW00425138

It's a Hell of a Life!

by Andrew Enzo Cocco

as told to Sandra Clitter

IT'S A HELL OF A LIFE!

Dedication

This book is dedicated to the woman who stood by my side for 62 years, my dear wife, Sara Cocco. She lived to see the book written, but not published, as she passed away on October 22, 2016. Many of the stories you'll read, she remembered, or reminded me to share.

With love to my dear Sara,

Andy

Forward

I have had the honor – and I don't use that word lightly – the true honor, to be given the opportunity to transcribe the life and stories of Andrew Enzo Cocco from verbal anecdotes to paper. This was not a task I sought. It wasn't something that I ever remotely thought of doing. For the record, I am NOT a writer. Apparently, however, the fact that I'm writing the forward to a book that I contributed to indicates that maybe I have assumed that mantle without realizing it.

I've known Mr. Cocco (no, I can NEVER call him 'Andy', although he loves the alliterative when he calls me on the phone and says 'Sandy, Andy here!') for 15 years – not nearly as long as most of the people in his life. We met because I frequent the Delco, PA Pizza chain that is his family's life work, called Cocco's Pizza. We got to know one another when he'd sit down with me to 'have a slice' (always asking me how my slice was – always doing quality control). Over those lunches, he told me a few stories from his life. I'd listen raptly because the stories were just fascinating.

Somewhere along the way, he mentioned that he wanted to write a book, to create his "memoirs". Like many other people had, I encouraged him to do just that. Mr. Cocco hired a few "real" writers, but for various reasons, walked away from those experiences frustrated. This summer, he called me and asked if I could help him get a court stenographer to sit down and record his stories. Of course, I'd be happy to, I responded. I did my research, got the information he needed and met him for lunch (yes, Mr. Cocco, the pizza was terrific!). I dutifully pulled out my notebook with all of the stenographic information that I'd gathered for him, but he sort of ignored me, and began telling me about Ferentino, Italy, the town in which he grew up. After about 10 minutes of listening, I looked him dead in the eye and said, "Am I supposed to be writing this all down?"

Well, since you're reading this, you will come to know Andrew Enzo Cocco (if you don't already). When I looked him in the eye,

I saw what I think of as the 'Santa Claus Twinkle' – you know what I mean, right? "Oh no," I think, "he wants ME to write this...I can't do it...I'm not a writer."

"Start writing," said Mr. Cocco. And he proceeded to tell me stories for about two hours. Trust me, I was scribbling as fast as I could. I don't take anything remotely like shorthand, so writing fast (and hopefully, legibly) was my only tool.

If you know this wonderful man, you also know that it is virtually impossible to say 'no' to him if he has his mind set on something. I gave in – but I DID have one condition.

My 'condition' was that he would read the first "Chapter" (we had about 10 pages of book written after that first session) the day that I brought it to him (not leaving it to sit on the dining room table for a week or two as he had done with other attempts on the book), and that if he didn't like it, we would part friends right then and there. It wasn't worth jeopardizing our friendship if I couldn't give him what he wanted. I wanted...no, I NEEDED, to know if he liked it...and I needed to know quickly.

He agreed to my condition. We parted ways after the first day of storytelling and I went back to my office to 'write'. I only struggled with what to write the first few moments...after that it flowed so easily...I realized that I just had to channel his storytelling through my fingers...that was all. The story itself is wonderful. It didn't need any help from me. It needed to be his voice, and I hope that we've managed – the two of us – to make that happen.

You've probably figured out that Mr. Cocco liked what he read in those first 10 pages. I was hired. We have had a multitude of "two-hour story sessions" since that first lunch. Those times are the times that I'll miss most, now that the book is done. Honestly, I never wanted it to end. When Mr. Cocco asked me if it was OK to add another story or make changes, I was eager, because it meant we'd be back together – in the Aston store, at Oak Avenue, in the Gelateria, or at his home, in his study or downstairs in the family room with his wonderful wife, Sara.

To the readers, may you thoroughly enjoy, for this is a gift to you from Mr. Cocco. It is a legacy of one man, but it is also a story of the opportunities presented by this great country in which we live.

Mr. Cocco, I have been honored to write your memoirs. I am awed by you, your accomplishments and your life. I am humbled by the fact that you trusted me with such a precious gift, for it was a gift – for me. Thank you for allowing me to be a small part of the process. You're absolutely right. Yours has been – and still is – a hell of a life!

With the deepest of affection and love,

Sandy

AGE 3

CARSWELL AIR FORCE BASE

GREAT-GRANDFATHER

LET'S SET THE STAGE

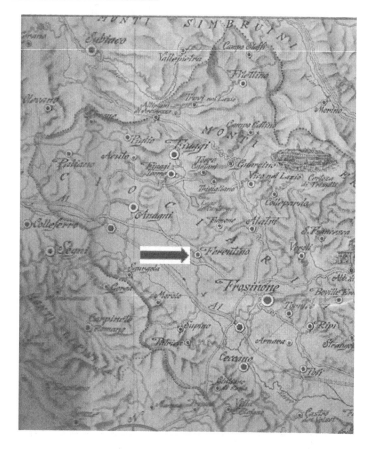

Ferentino, Italy

To understand who I am now, you have to understand who I was then and where I came from...way back then...in Italy in the early 1900's.

As they say, "my people" come from Ferentino, Italy, which is located about 40 miles southeast of Rome (in the province of Frosinone) and can trace its roots back to BC (as in "Before Christ").

Ferentino is the equivalent of the "county seat" in the U.S. It is situated on a hill about 1,300 feet above sea level. The higher the hill, the safer from invaders, for invaders would plow through lower towns on the way up the hill. Ferentino is high, but it isn't the highest.

Cathedral of Ferentino

Ferentino is a "walled city". The center of Ferentino (maybe a half mile across) was protected by the walls, though the town of Ferentino is larger than that – it includes farmland that surrounds those walls. Most everyone in the community lived inside the walls, but a few lived outside the walls and farmed or worked at the local paper factory. When Ferentino was attacked, everyone from the countryside would try to get into the walled portion of the city for protection.

The streets of Ferentino as they are today.

Attackers might get to the base of the hill outside of Ferentino, but they still had a heck of a climb to get up the hill, and those in Ferentino had the advantage of height in the attack. One of the doors to the city is called the "Blood Door", because when attacks would occur, the blood would run out that door and down the hill.

The walls of Ferentino are made without mortar – just one stone sitting on the other. This wall was built prior to the Roman Empire.

A double roman arch leading to Ferentino still stands today.

Today, there is a one-way road into Ferentino – a very narrow road, which you have to leave by another arch – via an equally narrow road. Obviously, the town was built way before cars and trucks ruled the roads.

The next town up the hill is Fumone. Fumone is smaller than Ferentino, but higher. The saying was "When Fumone smokes, the countryside shakes", because it meant that invaders had made it the entire way up the hill, and the situation wasn't good. The streets of Fumone are so narrow, that today, no cars are allowed inside the walls of the old city. It is strictly a pedestrian town.

But enough about the towns...back to my family...

My grandfather, Pasquale Cocco, had settled outside of the walls of Ferentino in the late 1800's, about three miles from the main road to town, five miles from the "city", and near a small paper factory.

My grandfather, Pasquale Cocco's, headstone.

There was a gravel path from the main road to the paper factory that was large enough for two oxen and a cart to move along slowly. Next to the factory was a creek. There was a reservoir near the factory, which was a fabulous place to swim.

The paper factory didn't make paper as we think of it today...they made brown paper bags out of chaff (the husks of corn or other seeds) and straw. The factory made its own electricity (since there wasn't any in the area) by burning coal, which was also used to heat the water. The straw was 'cooked' in hot water, and had two stones rotating through it, which 'ground' the wet straw into a paste. The paste was spread across a large (3' x 8') piece of felt and pressed between several small cylinders. As the paste advanced across the felt, the water in it drained off. When it reached the end of the felt, it went into a series of hot, metal cylinders, which pressed the paste into paper by forcing more of the water out. By the time it reached the last cylinder, it was dry paper, which was rolled and then sold.

Today, that factory would be thought of as ecologically advanced, but back then, it was a typical factory! Down the creek from the paper factory were three mills. These mills were where the corn, barley and wheat were ground into flour.

The small paper factory was about 200 yards from my grandfather's house. When people wanted to find the Cocco's, whomever they'd ask would say, "Up there, near the paper factory". Everyone knew the paper factory.

This is the paper factory as it stands today, but the process is the same, only the equipment has been modernized.

I'm using the term 'house' loosely – at least by modern standards. My grandfather's house had no running water. There was no electricity. There were four walls, a door, a fireplace, and a chimney. There were three rooms, including the kitchen.

You get the idea by now...this place, the home of my ancestors and my birthplace, was remote.

My grandfather was a shepherd, a farmer and owned a dry goods store. You might say that being an entrepreneur is in the Cocco's blood! We've always owned businesses.

The life of a shepherd is a hard one...it's a 24/7 job. You can't leave the sheep unattended, so, as they grazed the countryside, my grandfather would move with the sheep. Every day, the sheep would need to be milked, and the cheese made (Pecorino Cheese and Ricotta Cheese are made from sheep's milk). There would be a lambing season and a shearing season. As I said, being a shepherd is rough work.

As an aside, the cheese was made in a cauldron over a fire. The milk was heated, and branches from fig trees (green branches, which are "milky" if snapped) were added to the heated milk. The "milk" from the fig trees blended with the milk from the sheep and the curds formed!

Back to the sheep...Pasquale, my grandfather, had 300-400 sheep that he tended. He had two or three guys who worked for him moving with the herd as it grazed the countryside, and who participated in the milking, shearing and other sheep related chores.

Pasquale married Fravola, and together they had five children – Augusto, Luigi, Alfredo, and Angelina and Pietro who were twins.

As the boys grew up (because only boys would become the shepherds, girls would do the housework and raise the families), the boys would realize that they didn't want to live forever as a shepherd and would look for a way out of town.

Augusto found a way out of town by working for the Italian Railroad.

Luigi inherited the dry-goods store next to the paper factory from his father, and became a merchant.

Alfredo found a way out of town by moving to the United States and became a rock driller in New York City.

Angelina married and went to live in the town of Ferentino itself. She was a housewife and raised three boys including another set of twins.

And then there was Pietro...my father. Pietro (Peter) was born in 1899. He grew up in the "family business" (shepherding), just like his older brothers. When he got to the age of about 16 or 17, World War I entered the picture. Mussolini came to power. Fascism became the party of the land...but not for my father. My father was still working the land, still tending the sheep, but he also became a Socialist. Being a Socialist was not acceptable in Fascist Italy.

Mussolini made his key speeches from this square in Rome. (These days, my nephew owns the law firm 'Cocco Martini' right across the square! He has another office in Frosinone, too.)

Me beneath Mussolini's "Speaking Window".

At the age of 21, Pietro married Barbara, my mother. They lived with my grandparents and became the next generation to tend to the sheep. The family home, which had been just two rooms originally, had grown to accommodate the larger family, but there was still no electricity, still no running water...and it hadn't gotten any closer to the main road!

The house was, by now, three stories tall. The ground floor housed the kitchen, a storeroom and the dry goods store that my Uncle Luigi now ran. The second floor had my Uncle Luigi and his family in three rooms (there was something like nine people in that small space), plus two rooms were leased to tenants who worked at the paper factory. The third floor was our home. There were 26 steps to the third floor from the ground! We had part of the third floor (three rooms – a kitchen, a storeroom and a bedroom), and my grandfather had the other part. Altogether, there were 16 people living in this house!

Our House - after it expanded and expanded (this is 1995).

The store sold mostly dry goods (things that don't go bad), but it also sold some meats, like pepperoni or salami, which would keep without refrigeration. If you wanted some of those, you pointed to what you wanted, and my Aunt or Uncle hacked off a piece with a knife. You could also get beer and wine in the shop. My Aunt made pasta and bread in the rear of the store, and sold it in the front of the store.

The building on the left is where we stored the wood that we gathered all summer/fall, so that it would last us through the winter. The building on the right is the house. The bread was baked at the back of that structure on the right.

By 1922, Mussolini had become entrenched as Dictator, and the King of Italy became just a figurehead. Mussolini sent "enforcers" (aka "Blackshirts", so we weren't allowed to wear black shirts!) to every town to make sure that the citizens followed the Fascist doctrine.

My father was put in jail for a month or two – just for being a Socialist. When he was released, one of the guards (who happened to like my dad) told him to get out of Italy – not next year, not next month, but RIGHT NOW. Don't go home. Leave today. The guard promised to (and did) get word to my mother that my father was on his way to safety, outside of Italy.

The back of the house as it was in 1995.

As the guard was telling my father to "get going", my dad saw the police come into the piazza where he stood with the guard. My dad took off, heading for the Porta Sanguinaria door (each of the doors in the city has a name). He ran and ran, trying to get away from the police. As he went down one street, he realized that he was becoming tired, and that they were going to catch him. He saw a woman knitting in an open door. He headed her way. As he ran by, through the open door, he said to her, "They're after me. Please don't tell them that I came in here." A few minutes later, the cops came and paused at her door. "Did you see a guy?" She calmly replied, "I saw a guy running, but he went past quickly." Pietro was safe. He got to the door of the city.

A typical street in Ferentino...Dad ran through streets like these to escape the Blackshirts.

Once outside, there were few homes, so he ran until he was able to hop on a train somewhere in the countryside, and managed to escape.

**This is the door, Porta Sanguinara, through which my
dad, Pietro, escaped.**

Pietro made his way to Genoa, the largest shipping port in Italy,
and wangled a job on a merchant ship heading to the United
States. He landed in New York City (well, actually, he jumped
ship to avoid immigration because he didn't have the proper
paperwork), and found his brother, Alfredo, who lived in in
Brooklyn with his family. Pietro became Peter in the United
States.

Lo and behold, Barbara was pregnant when Pietro went to jail and later left for America. Barbara stayed with my grandfather, Pasquale. Pasquale gave her a little land (a couple of acres) to farm that she leased out to sharecroppers for a portion of the harvest (wheat and corn). Pasquale expanded the house a little to accommodate my mother and the growing family.

My oldest brother, Leandro, was born in December 1922. My father was in the United States when he was born. My mother and brother lived with my grandparents back in Ferentino.

Dad didn't come back to Italy until 1926. He had said that he was going to earn some money, then come back to Italy and buy some land, but he never came back for more than a visit. Some guys came home and stayed, but with my father, it was just a pretense. He liked New York too much to leave.

He did send some money home from New York from time to time. Every few years, he came home to work the land and make sure everything was OK, then he headed back to the United States on May 1, 1927, after staying in Italy for about a year. Pietro went through Ellis Island after that trip home, thus becoming an 'official' immigrant, even though he wasn't a citizen yet.

Since my father had gone back to Italy in 1926, my second brother, Americo, was born in 1927!

Pietro Cocco applied to become a U.S. citizen in 1928 and became fully naturalized on October 3, 1929.

In New York, Peter was working with a construction firm by the name of Collins Construction. Dad was a rock-driller (Uncle Alfredo was a rock-driller and helped Dad get the job), working on some of the most famous landmarks in New York City including the Empire State Building, the Lincoln Tunnel and Rockefeller Center, among other landmarks.

No. 3145845

Name .... **COCCO, PETER** ....

residing at .... **261 West 15th St., New YorkCity** ....

Age .. **30** .... years. Date of order of admission .... **OCT 3 1929** ....

Date certificate issued .... **OCT 3 1929** .... by the

.. **U.S.Dist.** .... Court at .... **New York.** ....

Petition No. **147312**

Peter Cocco

(Complete and true signature of holder)

My father's naturalization record.

The working conditions were awful. The drillers were supposed to wear masks, but the masks hampered their work, so they would only wear them if they knew (and they always knew) that an inspector was coming. They got much more work done without the masks. None of the rock-drillers of the time lived much past 55 years old.

Back in Italy, Mussolini was still firmly in power. His goal was to make every person literate, so he mandated that all children attend first through fourth grades. Most of these "schools" were rented rooms in a home – one room for all the children attending that school. Once a kid in my area completed 4th grade, it was difficult to continue with school because the school that had 5th grade was in town – five miles away.

My mother made sure that my eldest brother went to 5th grade...she sent him to Alatri (five miles from the town of Ferentino), to stay and study in a seminary, and to get a good education.

My second brother started school in 1933 and moved on to the seminary once he completed 4th grade, as well. The seminary that he attended was in Frascati, about 30 miles from home.

Sending my brothers to the seminary took most of the cash my mother was able to accumulate, but my brothers both got a very good education. To pay for the room and board, my brothers both tutored.

Well, Dad came back to Italy again in 1932 and, you guessed it, I was born in 1933. I am Enzo Cocco...and this is my story...

My birth certificate (well, a duplicate from 1969).

THE EARLY YEARS

I was born October 17, 1933. In Italy, your godparents play a very important role in your life. In fact, it is so important that they actually name you. My godparents were Vincenzo and Nina Zacchari. Accordingly, I was named 'Enzo', a form of 'Vincenzo', in honor of my godfather. Because we were five miles from the Cathedral in Ferentino, I wasn't baptized (and my birth recorded) until three or four months after I was born. At that time, the Zacchari's took me to Ferentino to get me baptized and register my birth. When they did this, they actually gave the wrong date to the church – October 23, 1933. Take your pick...I'll celebrate either day!

My earliest memory is of waking up crying, though I didn't have a sad childhood. My mother came in and said, "Enzo, Ninu (an endearment for 'sweetie'), why are you crying? Here are some fresh-picked grapes with the dew still on them." That is my oldest, and one of my fondest, memories.

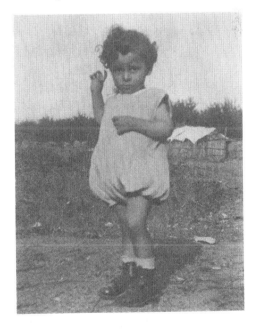

Me at age 3.

Another early memory is of a time with my grandfather. By this time, Pasquale was up in years. He'd sit in his chair and smoke stogies (cigars) all day. One day, he leaned over and put his stogie in my mouth. When I took a puff, I coughed and coughed and coughed. I did NOT like it! My mother saw her father-in-law do this, and just blasted the heck out of him. That was the last stogie for me!

I had a wonderful childhood. I was growing up in a Socialist house, in a Fascist country, but I didn't know that. In addition to numerous other chores, I was responsible for taking care of the pig (we killed one-a-year – more on the pigs later), and the rabbits. I had to find rabbit food...we didn't have PetSmart down the road to buy rabbit pellets. I had to gather the grasses and leaves that the rabbits liked. Sometimes, I'd steal my mother's lettuce – a real treat for the rabbits. I don't think that pleased my mother.

The view of Ferentino from our house.

My school was 200 yards from my house, at my friend, Loreto (Larry) Palumbo's, house. One room of his parents' house was the "schoolhouse"...that one room was where all the kids in our area attended 1st to 4th grade. Our teacher for all of those years was Signora Cervigni (Sidenote: Later, when I returned to Italy for a visit, I got to meet/visit with her daughter!).

The mile circle around our house was my playground. My mother didn't have to worry about me being hit by a car or getting hurt...there was nothing around!

Our life revolved around the sun. When the sun went down, you went in. When it rose, your work day started.

The view of Morolo from our house (the sea is on the other side of the mountain).

THE HARVEST

Harvest time for the wheat and corn was the highlight of my year. We grew what we needed to supply our family with grain (corn or wheat) until the next harvest.

When it was time to harvest the wheat, all of the families in the area pooled their resources and hired a thresher. The thresher was pulled by a tractor, down that three-mile path from the main gravel road (which was fairly passable), down to the paper factory and on to the "rink" (a solid piece of cement surrounded

IT'S A HELL OF A LIFE!

by curb). The trek down the path took a half-day with guys going ahead and behind the tractor to fill in the potholes in the path, so that neither piece of equipment would get stuck in the ruts. Watching that procession was like watching the Macy's Thanksgiving Day Parade in Ferentino. Some of my happiest days were the days that the thresher arrived. I never missed the arrival of the thresher, because it made such noise coming in that you could hear it all through the hills.

Once the thresher had made its way down the path, into the "neighborhood", it was parked at the Celani family's house. This was my mother's family. They owned the most ground in the area. They even had cows. The Celanis got the privilege of having the thresher park in the "rink" outside of their house. The tractor parked outside the rink, and a long belt ran between the tractor and the thresher. The tractor powered the thresher, which separated the wheat from the chaff, then sent the straw out the back-end to be baled. The wheat was gathered, and we had the beginning of our provisions for the winter ahead.

The harvesting of the corn meant a totally different process. After the corn matured, we went through the fields and pulled all of the ears off of the stalk. Once the mature ears of corn were cut off, the corn was husked (the outside "leaves" removed), leaving only the corn cob (with kernels attached) behind. Don't worry, the stalk and husk didn't go to waste. The stalks were cut down with a scythe after the ears were removed. Then, the stalk was cut up and put in a pile in the back of the house to become cattle feed. We didn't have any silos. The corn cobs (after the corn was removed) were also thrown into this pile to help to feed the animals through the winter.

The "leaves" of the corn gave me a new mattress! Yes, my mattress was a sack filled with corn leaves. Once a year, I'd dump out the old leaves (which were nothing but dust by September or October) and fill it back up with fresh corn leaves. For a while, I'd have a very plump mattress...at least until it began disintegrating again.

P a g e | 22

Shucking the corn was actually fun. This was a chore that was done by the women and kids. The families would hire an accordion player who would sit in the middle of the circle and would play traditional Italian songs. We'd sing and shuck the corn. Each one of us had a pile of ears of corn. Once an ear was shucked, the "clean" ear would be thrown into the center of the "rink" and left in the sun to dry. Someone would "stir" the corn occasionally, so that all of the ears of corn got sunlight and exposure to the air. This allowed the ears of corn to dry, so that we could remove the kernels of corn.

Separating the kernels from the corn cob ("shelling the corn") itself isn't easy. Fresh corn is impossible to separate from the cob, which is why we dried it first. Once the corn was dry (after it had baked in the sun for a while), the men used a homemade tool (wooden) to "beat" the pile of dried cobs. They would fling the tool through the pile, and the kernels would fall away! It was magic! Two men would use a "beater" on the same pile at the same time, and they never hit each other. The kernels would pop off of the cob. A third man would turn the cobs, "stirring" the pile. The corn would fall to the bottom, and the "naked" cobs would be shoveled out of the pile. The corn kernels themselves would then be shoveled into sacks.

All of this work gave each family two to three sacks of corn. That corn (and the wheat that was threshed) had to last us until the next harvest.

Some of the corn cobs would be infected with worms. Not even those cobs went to waste. It was my job to dig the worms out of the rotten cobs. I'd drop the worms in a jar, then use those worms as bait for trapping birds. Yes, trapping birds (more on that later).

After the wheat was threshed, or the corn was separated from the cob, those seeds were kept whole until we needed flour. You wouldn't grind it early, as it would spoil or become home to insects and mice. When you needed flour or cornmeal, you took the seed to one of the three mills along the creek and got it ground.

Grinding seeds down to flour requires a large grindstone and a lot of water to turn the wheel that moves the grindstone. Each mill along the creek had its own reservoir which held a good amount of water until it was time to turn the wheel. When the water was released, the wheel would turn.

Since there were three mills along the creek, and water was precious, the top mill would ring a bell when it was going to release water to grind flour. That would alert the second mill that their reservoir would be filling up, and they could grind, too.

Without much cash, we would often pay for the grinding by paying the mill with a portion of the new flour. We got some and they kept some, which they would then sell in town.

Our vegetable garden provided all the produce we needed – fresh during the summer – but we needed some for the winter, as well.

To make the tomato sauce (gravy), my mother would take the ripe tomatoes from the garden and cook them for a while to boil off the extra water in the tomatoes and make the resulting mess thicker. When the tomatoes were cooked down, they were spread over a large wooden board (about 4'x 6'), and set in the sun to dry.

It was my job to go out once a day and 'turn' the paste. Using a long spatula, I'd flip all of the tomato sauce on the board. I'd do this every day until it was hard (dry) enough to make a ball about the size of a baseball, or a little smaller. Once the tomato paste had been formed into balls, they were placed in a jar and the jar was then filled with olive oil. That tomato paste wouldn't spoil all winter.

When my mother wanted to make a sauce ("sugo", in Italian), she'd take out all the herbs she'd need for seasoning and a bit of lard, and beat those into a paste. That paste melted like oil. She'd add a ball or two of tomato and cook it until it was a delicious sauce.

We gathered Porcini mushrooms (much better than Portobello mushrooms!) in the fall. We'd go along looking for the mushrooms, using a stick to turn over the leaves and make sure there were no snakes lurking, before we'd reach down to cut the mushrooms. We'd take our haul home. My mother would use some right away (fresh), but some were to be dried to be used throughout the year. The mushrooms to be dried were strung using a needle and thread and hung from the ceiling rafters in the storeroom to dry.

We had a grove of chestnut trees about a half mile away. During harvest time, we'd gather the chestnuts, which we could roasted over the fire in the winter.

Grapes were harvested in September. We'd cut large bunches of grapes, and, like the mushrooms, we'd hang them on a string from the ceiling in the storeroom. They would last until April and still be good grapes – they wouldn't have shrunk down to raisins yet!

Apples, pears and potatoes were stored on a bed of straw in the loft of the storage room. The straw helped to prevent them from rotting and sprouting during the winter. Flour, wheat, corn, and beans were stored here, as well.

That storeroom had all kinds of food hanging from the ceiling – sausage, prosciutto, grapes, mushroom, herbs – most of the food we needed to last us through the winter and into the next year.

THE HUNTING

In order to trap birds, I had to, well, build traps. I'd go down to the paper factory and pick up some of the wire that held the bales together before they were processed into paper. I straightened out the wire, then made traps out of the wire, and used the worms to bait the traps. I got so good at making these traps that I'd sell the extras to my buddies for two or three eggs a trap (not to get ahead of my story, but when I left Italy, I left behind over 150 traps). If I got too many eggs, I'd go to the dry goods store that my Uncle Luigi owned and sell the eggs to him for candy or other treats.

One of my favorite treats to "buy" with my eggs was brioski, which you added to water to get "fizzy water" (kind of like modern "seltzer").

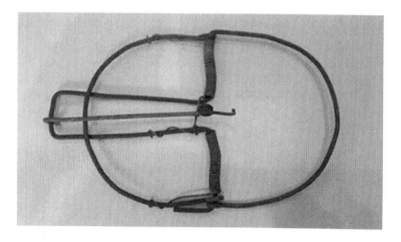

One of my homemade traps – this one is set (a worm would be tied to the little "hook" in the middle to lure the bird).

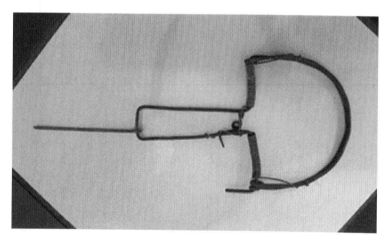

Once the trap 'springs', then the bird would be caught between the 'jaws' of the trap.

I'd blend the trap into the surrounding dirt, so that the trap sort of blended in and the bird could only see the worm tied by its tail (yes, I could tell the head from the tail!) to the hook. I'd go around checking all my traps every hour. I usually caught 10 or 15 each time I set the traps. When I caught a bird (it would die in the trap), I'd put its head through my string belt (we didn't have leather belts) until I had birds hanging all around my waist! I caught migratory birds we called 'castriche', but I also caught blackbirds. The prime trapping time was around the harvest.

Pigeons would nest under the eaves of the house. When we could, we'd catch them and eat the squabs. Those were a treat!

My mother would say to me, "Enzo, go out and get me a couple of birds, so that I can make some sauce." Can you imagine making sauce out of birds?

In the spring, I'd be sent down to the creek ("Enzo, why don't you go down to the creek and see if you can get some snails.") with a bucket, right after a rain shower, when the sun came back out. I'd look for large leaves growing near the creek. If you peeked under the leaves, right after the rain, you could find snails there. In about an hour, I would catch four or five dozen snails and stick them in the bucket.

I'd take the bucket home and cover it – tightly – so that the snails couldn't escape. Once I got there, I'd transfer the snails into a bushel basket, so that they could 'breathe'. We'd feed the snails in the basket for four or five days. In that time, the snails would actually take on the flavor of whatever you fed them and stop being 'snailey'. We'd feed the snails cornmeal, so after four or five days, when they were cooked (shell and all) and served over pasta in a nice tomato sauce, they tasted like corn! This was a real delicacy. The French have nothing on the Italians with their escargot.

We could get different, smaller snails in the summer by turning rocks over. You'd find five or six snails under a rock. You'd have 10 dozen snails in no time. These weren't the "special" snails, these were more "regular" snails. Even so, we'd catch them and feed them, Mom would cook them, and we'd have a treat!

THE SLAUGHTER

We would plant and we would harvest, but we also raised our animals. In our case, we raised a pig, chickens and rabbits.

I was in charge of the rabbits. When we needed more rabbits, I would put the male rabbit in the cage with the female rabbit. Thirty or thirty-one days later, we'd have more rabbits! The rabbits were used primarily for meat, but it was my responsibility to care for them and fatten them up.

If we ended up with more rabbits than we could use, then I'd give them to my uncle who would take them into town and sell them, then he'd give me the money. He didn't take live rabbits to town. The carcasses would hang from a hook, and the people would choose the ones that they wanted from the selection.

Remember, without electricity and refrigeration, food (unless it was preserved) had to be eaten right away. The rabbits that were killed in the morning were probably on someone's dish that night.

The chickens were important for the eggs and for the meat. Sometime in February, one or two of the hens would "get a fever". They would become listless and stop eating. That period lasted for about a month. We would save all of the eggs produced by all the hens during that period, and we'd put them under a brood chicken to hatch. If the eggs had been fertilized, then we would have chicks in about three weeks. If there weren't enough chicks produced, then that poor rooster would become Sunday dinner.

By far, the most important animal we owned was the pig. The annual pig provided us much of the meat that we would have during the year – some of the best meat. Each year, I would be given a piglet to raise. That piglet would grow into an adult and follow me all around as I went through my days. As we approached the time for the slaughter, the pig would be confined to a stall – to get fed well and get fat – literally.

We slaughtered in November once the air got cool. Without refrigeration, we couldn't keep meat fresh, so we needed nature's own preservative – the fall/winter and salt – to help us keep our meat from spoiling. My mother's brother-in-law (her sister's husband), Uncle Mike, was a butcher. Uncle Mike would show up in November with his sharp knife. Three or four men would hold the pig down on a plank, and Uncle Mike, very skilled at his craft, would stick the pig, killing him quickly and mercifully.

After the pig was dead, a torch and knife were used to scrape all of the hair off of the pig.

Once it was "naked", it was hung in the kitchen (head down). A cut was made down the center, and all of the entrails were removed. The intestines were cleaned and sterilized in hot water, and used for sausage casing. The blood was captured and saved to make blood sausage. That pig hung in the kitchen for three days – it couldn't be cut until rigor mortis set in. Only then could the meat be harvested.

Obviously, the carcass attracted flies by the thousands. You couldn't have them going into the open pig, laying eggs and destroying the meat. How did we stop that from happening? Nothing on that pig was thrown away. Believe it or not, it was the pig's own lungs that were removed and cut open to form a net that covered the carcass and kept the flies out. The pig actually provided its own protective netting.

When it was time to cut up the carcass, they started at the lowest part which was now the head. The head was used to make Guanciale (Italian pronunciation: [gwan'tʃaːle]), which is an Italian cured meat or salami product prepared from pork jowl or cheeks.

During this time, the fire in the kitchen hearth was built-up and burned full-blast. A cauldron hung over the fire. As the fat was cut from the pig, it was thrown into the cauldron to melt and cook down for lard (what we think of now as Crisco) and pork rinds.

Some of the fat was poured off into 1 ½" x 10" x 12" pans. Lye was added. This was our soap. We only took enough fat to melt down for soap to give us enough soap for the next year.

The rest of the lard was saved for cooking.

The pig's legs became prosciutto once it had been salted and cured 'just so'.

Prior to the slaughter of the pig, we would trade some of our corn or wheat for salt. Each family used about 50 pounds of salt to preserve the meat, or to add to the lard (so it wouldn't go rancid), and finally, to spice the prosciutto and bacon.

Once the meat was prepared, it would be laid into a large wooden crate. One layer of meat, one layer of salt, and so on. When it was all secure, the lid would be sealed with weights. Preserving the meat properly was critical because that meat had to last us until the next pig was raised/slaughtered.

Prosciutto was the best of the best of the meat, and was given special attention. Before being stored in the crate, the joints were stuffed with hot peppers – to further deter any fly larvae from developing and spoiling the meat.

Once the crate was sealed, the meat would cure for the winter. We had to wait three to four months to see (and taste) the fruits of our labor. Come April or May, we feasted!

I vividly remember the first time my "pet" went to "meet" Uncle Mike. I was shocked and upset, however in time, I learned to get over it for a couple of reasons: First, I learned that wonderful food would follow, and about a week after the killing, a new piglet arrived, and the process would begin all over again.

RANDOM THOUGHTS ON DAILY LIFE

Breakfast usually consisted of toast, coffee and milk.

We would draw our water up from a well, but it wasn't purified water like we have today. It had animal waste in it, among other things, so we couldn't drink it. The well-water was used for cooking and cleaning. We had a spring not too far from the house that we used for drinking water. Our fireplace was burning constantly – winter and summer. My mother cooked every meal on the fire in the kitchen.

In the springtime, she would feed the sharecroppers who worked the land (which they dug with a "vanga" (a "spade" in English) – we didn't have tractors). She would cook, then carry the pot outside, and the two of us would eat with the sharecroppers. The pot would go on the ground, the sharecroppers would cover the ground with a cloth, everyone would grab a spoon, and we'd have a picnic. You'd just dig into the pot. The faster you ate, the more food you got!

Doing the laundry was a lot harder than it is today. My mother would take the dirty clothes (you had to wear the same clothes for a couple of weeks, but you swam in your clothes during the nice weather, so it wasn't all that bad...winter was worse) and put them in a cauldron of hot water filled about half way. After the clothes had "cooked", she'd move them from the cauldron into a bushel basket, which was lined with a sheet or piece of cloth. She soaped the clothes in the bushel basket. When she was done soaping them (and scrubbing them), she'd wrap the sheet around the clothes. She'd take the coals from the fireplace and put them in hot water to make hot ashes. Then, she'd dump that mixture on top of the sheet (on top of the bundle of clothes). The hot water would drain through the clothes, cleaning and purifying them, and the ash residue would stay on the outside of the sheet. When that process was done, the bundle of clothes would be put in the basket, and she'd carry the basket – on her head – down to the creek to rinse out (and scrub on a flat rock, if more scrubbing was necessary). When the clothes were rinsed, she'd carry them back to the house in the basket, and hang them outside on the line, to dry.

A tailor came every three or four months, or so, to help with alterations to existing clothes, or making new clothes. He arrived on his bike, which he had to push the last two or three miles because our path was so rutted. His sewing machine strapped to the bike. Remember, we didn't have electricity, so the sewing machine was a pedal machine. He's set up shop on the bocce court and would mend anything that people brought to him. If you wanted something new, he'd take the measurements, and the cloth (or the old clothes which were to be "transformed") with him, then bring back the finished pieces the next time he came around. Most of our clothes were made from older clothes. New fabric or truly new clothes were a luxury we could rarely afford.

Sara Cocco at Mom's clothesline in 1995.

Uncle Luigi's store sold dry goods, beer and wine. My grandfather would take the cheese (that he'd made from the sheep's milk) to town in a two-wheeled cart (and pulled by a mule) and sell the cheese for dry goods to stock the store. The store served the families right in our 'neighborhood', and the workers from the paper factory. The beer was kept cold in a 'cave' outside the store. Remember, where you don't have electricity or running water, you also don't have ice!

With no electricity or running water, we were outside from dawn till dusk. When we came in at night and sat by the fire, our mother checked our heads for lice! Talk about fun! We had kerosene candles, but they gave off very little light.

**My mother, Barbara (left),
and her sister, my Aunt Anna.**

When the weather was nice, the men in the area would gather in front of the store at night to play bocce on the packed dirt until it became dark. After dark, they'd play "Morra". Morra is a game played only with the hands. You can have any number of players. Each player reveals their hand – with some number of fingers extended – at the same time. The player who guesses the total number of fingers that will be extended scores a point. The men could play Morra for hours on end. In reality, this was really just a drinking game.

The kids invented all kinds of games to keep ourselves amused. We didn't have board games or video games or anything else like that. We had to make up our games.

Peach stones (peach pits) were our 'currency'. We bet with our peach pits, so having a big bag of them made you 'rich'. We would make piles of peach stones – little stacks – then walk a little ways away and throw a larger stone at the pile and try to knock it down. If you succeeded in knocking the stack down, then you won the entire pile. So, having a big stone to throw at the pile was important. You'd guard your larger stones!

We used to have foot races around the creek that ran by the paper factory. The paper factory burned coal, and they dumped the ashes from the coal into the creek. One day, I decided to take a shortcut and run through the ashes in the creek, rather than going over the little bridge crossing that we had. WELL! Little did I know that the ashes were still hot, and I burned the bottom of my feet terribly. I hobbled home to show my mother. My mother took one look at the blistered soles of my feet, then slapped me across my mouth. Then, she hugged me, sat me down, and began to "doctor" my burns. She put my feet in cool water, sliced potatoes very thin, and applied them to the bottom of my feet. She proceeded to wrap my feet in rags. She'd change those bandages every day. I couldn't do anything for three days, but sit in a chair, but by the time she removed the rags on the 3rd day, my feet were healed. No scars. Nothing. It was like it didn't happen. We couldn't go to doctors...we only had the natural remedies passed down from generation to generation.

As I grew, maybe when I was about seven or eight, I became jealous of a cousin of mine who was a shepherd. It was a treat for me to be allowed to go out with him as his sheep grazed the countryside. You slept under the stars, tending the sheep.

When I got to go out with the sheep, breakfast was a favorite meal of mine. We'd dunk a crust of hard-bread in whey (the watery part of the sheep's milk that is left after the curds are formed for the cheese), then put fresh ricotta on top. Now THAT was a good breakfast!

My mother made it very clear that no son of hers was going to be a shepherd (after all, she'd sent my older brothers to the seminary to avoid just that fate). To try to pacify me and get me off of the shepherd "kick", she allowed me to raise a lamb. The only problem was that the lamb was actually a ram. As he grew up, he became aggressive. One day, I was cutting grass (to feed the rabbits), and I turned around to see him pawing the ground. That's a signal of aggression. I took off as fast as I could, but I ran up against a ditch. I paused on the edge of the ditch – just long enough to get my balance to try and jump across – but the ram reached me first and "helped" me over the ditch by hitting me on the butt with his head/horns. Very shortly thereafter, my ram became part of our dinner.

Without running water, baths were a luxury. In the summer, we would simply go to the creek to bathe. In the winter, however, when the water was too cold to swim, we would bathe – maybe once a month - in a galvanized, five-gallon tub. First, you'd cart the water from outside, up the 26 stairs to the house. Mom would heat the water over the fire. Then, you'd strip down and stand in the tub. She'd pour the hot water over you to get you wet. You'd soap yourself thoroughly (with the homemade soap), then she'd pour more hot water on you to wash it away. When you only bathe once a month, you can actually see layers of skin washing off your body. Skin rejuvenates in a month, so you were getting rid of all of the "old" skin. Kind of like a snake!

For the first 10 years of my life, this cycle repeated itself. As I grew, my responsibilities grew, but each year was basically the same – there was a planting, a harvest, a slaughter, a winter. There was school, there was play, there were chores. Despite the fact that it sounds fairly primitive compared to today, it was really an idyllic life and I had a ball!

My First Holy Communion – age 9-ish.

I am happy that this was my life. Everything beautiful was around you. You didn't hear traffic or other noises. Nothing but nature. It was kind of like *Swiss Family Robinson*, but we weren't stranded on an island!

ROME

Imagine being 10 years old and never having seen running water, indoor plumbing or electricity. Imagine having two older brothers who you rarely saw because they lived away from home in the seminary. Imagine never having been more than a few miles from your home.

My brothers pretty much didn't exist for me before I was 10...but the year I was 10, my life changed.

My brother Leandro had been drafted into the Army as a 2nd

Lieutenant directly from the seminary back around 1939. The Army took everyone who had been to the seminary because they knew that these young men had good educations. Leandro ended up commanding troops. He knew what was going on – not good things. When the Armistice was signed, the Italian Army effectively disbanded and Leandro came home.

When Leandro came back he was a grown man. He tried his hand at selling shoe polish to stores, but that didn't last long. He started selling insurance for Allianz. He bought a Vespa. His career was launched. He sold insurance for his entire career.

It was 1943. I wasn't really aware of it, but World War II was coming to our doorstep.

My brother Americo was sent home from the seminary in June 1943 because they didn't have enough food for the students. Out in the country where we lived, we really didn't have any food shortages because we grew most of it ourselves.

When I asked why there wasn't food at the seminary, I was told that there was a war on (that was news to me!), and that the United States, Italy, Germany, Russian, France, and England were all fighting.

June 1943 is the first time that I remember living under the same roof as one of my brothers (I was four when Americo went to the seminary in the first place, and Leandro was already gone, so I don't remember them being around).

Remember, we had a small house – three rooms. The first room was the kitchen with the smokey fireplace. The second was the room where we stored all of our provisions. It was sort of a pantry. The third room was the bedroom. It had two beds. Everyone slept in the one bedroom.

When Americo came home from the seminary, he got the extra bed, and I had to bunk with my mother. My brother was 16, and liked to sleep late because he'd stay out late at night (face it, he was 16, he wanted to be out with his friends, not sitting around with his mother and kid brother). I was an early riser. Americo had been home two weeks when I'd had enough (at the ripe old age of 10) of his sleeping in, so I grabbed a pillow and began hitting him with it. He took the pounding the first day, but by the second day, he was ready for me.

Americo grabbed the pillow that I'd just swung and pulled – hard. His elbow hit my eye and forehead. He hit it so hard, that there was blood everywhere. Blood was gushing out of my left eye, but it stopped fairly quickly. My mother treated the cuts with her remedies, and the external injuries began to heal. My eye, however, well that was another story. My eye itself began to "bleed". The inside wasn't healing, even if the outside was. My family was afraid that I would lose my eye if it wasn't examined by a specialist, so, my mother sent me to Rome.

It was June 1943. My life changed forever.

My godparents lived in Rome. My mother packed my brother, Americo, and me onto a train for the 30-mile journey to Rome. Remember, I'd never been more than a few miles from my home. The walk TO the train actually took longer than the ride ON the train!

As the train headed northwest I started seeing different things. For the first time in my life I saw a **WHOLE NEW WORLD**!!!

Arriving in Rome, I saw things I never imagined existed: music, newspapers, radio, indoor plumbing, faucets, bidets, electricity, and the telephone. Horseless carriages (cars), cobbled streets, kids on roller skates, bicycles, and airplanes.

My godparents lived outside of the Vatican, and my godfather worked for the Vatican.

My godmother, and cousin, Nina.

The gate to the Vatican (today).

Of course, I wasn't here to sightsee, but I was soaking it all in. I was taken to the doctor every two or three days. My eye was saved. For me, however, my eye wasn't the big thing about the trip to Rome. To me, the most memorable part of the trip was seeing and experiencing all the new things – everything that Rome had to offer.

Because of the war, there was rationing, which caused shortages on all kinds of household items. There would be lines outside of stores, where people would wait, hoping that they'd be able to purchase something before the store ran out.

Since my godfather worked in the Vatican, we could shop at the Vatican store. The Vatican store was NOT on rationing, so we were always able to buy these precious items. One of my "jobs" while I was in Rome was to go over to the store every day and pick up a quart of milk, a loaf of bread, and anything else that we needed at the house. I'd charge it to my godfather's account, and the purchases would be deducted from his wages.

I'd take the tram or the trolley all over the city. I had an aunt on the other side of Rome, so I'd go over there to visit and soak up all the sights along the way. I went to visit the Colosseum. I drank it all in.

Americo had gone home (back to Ferentino) shortly after we got to Rome. I stayed for five or six weeks during the late summer of 1943. I was there for August into September.

It was in Rome that I began to understand that there was a war swirling around Italy. World War II was raging and I never knew it being 10-years-old and living in Ferentino.

My first exposure to the war was the air raid siren. During the first night in Rome, the air raid siren sounded. We all trooped to the basement where there was a shelter. "What's going on?" I asked. "There's a war on," was the response. I never knew. Somehow, I never knew.

I slept on the couch in my godparents' apartment. It took me a while to figure out that every loud sound was NOT an air raid. One night, I thought I'd heard the air raid siren, and I raced to the basement...only to find out that I was the only one racing. When I went to get everyone else, they assured me that the loud sound that I'd heard was NOT an air raid siren, but rather the popping of a transformer.

There were two "real" air raid drills while I was in Rome, and we made our way, safely, to the basement bunker.

As summer turned to fall, I returned to Ferentino – my injured eye had healed, and now both of my eyes were WIDE OPEN. Oh, the things that I had seen. I was AMAZED!

WORLD WAR II COMES TO FERENTINO

Before I really get into the "War Years", I want to mention my father again. As you may have noticed, my father doesn't figure in the stories of my first 10 years. My father came back to Ferentino occasionally, but he always left and went back to America – alone. While many men left their families to go searching for a better life, they usually saved to bring their families over to America with them. My father was living relatively well in New York, and his family was back in Ferentino living in a house with no amenities, little money and cut off from modern life – in other words, dirt poor. This just wasn't right. It wasn't right that he was living well in New York, and we were living so "rough" back in Italy.

As World War II began brewing in Italy, Dad made another trip to Ferentino. It was probably 1938 when he came home.

Dad was still in Ferentino in early 1939. Many U.S. immigrants took the opportunity before the war to get their families out of Fascist Italy before it began. If you were a U.S. citizen (and my father was by that time), then you could bring your family into the United States. It was a golden opportunity to move your family to a better life.

Instead, my father left – again – without his family. Around this time, I remember my mother saying that the United States recalled its citizens back home due to the "world situation". She was probably explaining to me why my father had left. Pietro arrived back in New York April 6, 1939 – without his family.

I have to ask: What makes a man do that? What kind of a person does that?

As an adult, I can certainly hazard a guess, but I won't let those thoughts cross my lips. My mother didn't talk about it at all. I am angry about his selfishness even today. Very angry.

He could have brought us out – prior to the war. We could have been in school. We could have learned the language. His wife would have had a home with heat, water and utilities. How could he just leave us there?

My dad, Peter, in New York in 1939.

My mother deserved a medal for what she went through, and the grace with which she dealt with the situation. She had to be angry and resentful, but she

NEVER passed that feeling along to me. She never said a bad thing about my father to me or in front of me, yet she HAD to have had some very strong feelings.

What kind of a guy is living a life like the one in the photo above, while his family, his wife and three kids back in Italy, are living in a home without electricity and indoor plumbing?

My father, Peter, in the U.S. Army

The 1940 Census shows my father living in Brooklyn as a boarder.

Since Dad was living in the United States when World War II arrived, he was drafted in 1942 (at 43 years old). Because of his age, they didn't send him to the front lines. He started at a base where they were making bombs. He said later that he would wonder if any of the bombs that he handled would kill one of his children back in Italy. They made him a welder, and there he remained for the rest of the war.

Name:	Peter Cocco
Birth Year:	1899
Race:	White, citizen (White)
Nativity State or Country:	Italy or San Marino
State of Residence:	New York
County or City:	Kings
Enlistment Date:	13 Jul 1942
Enlistment State:	New York
Enlistment City:	Fort Jay Governors Island
Branch Code:	Branch Immaterial - Warrant Officers, USA
Grade:	Private
Grade Code:	Private
Term of Enlistment:	Enlistment for the duration of the War or other emergency, plus six months, subject to the discretion of the President or otherwise according to law
Component:	Selectees (Enlisted Men)
Source:	Civil Life
Education:	Grammar school
Civil Occupation:	Semiskilled drillers, extraction of minerals and construction
Marital Status:	Separated, without dependents

My father's Enlistment Record.

Enough of that...on with the story...

After my trip to Rome, I arrived back in Ferentino in September of 1943. We were approaching the time of the harvest and the slaughter of the pig.

Not long after I returned to Ferentino from Rome, I found a large lump on my groin. When I told my mother, she went down to the creek and found a particular type of leaves. She boiled them down and made a paste which she spread over the lump and covered it. She changed this dressing six or seven times a day for a couple of days. Incredibly, the lump just disappeared. It was like it had never been there.

In late September, I began hearing planes flying over or close to our house. A railroad bridge three miles away was a prime target of the Allies. They would fly over the bridge every day and try to bomb it. Every day they missed! They NEVER hit it!

After a while, I actually started heading across the countryside to get a better view of the bombings. They were such a part of life, that I treated them as my entertainment, rather than being frightened of the war. If I had had a watch, I could have set it for 10 a.m. as the B-25 or B-26 planes flew overhead every day.

We would run for cover when the daily bombings began. I had a cousin who was killed by a bomb, but mostly they weren't too close. I found it interesting, after I got used to them, to watch the dogfights between the American B-51's and the German planes. One of them would get shot down, and you would see them parachute to the ground. If the pilot was someone from the Allied side of the war, you couldn't try to hide them because if the Germans found out you were doing that, they would kill you and your family.

The war had begun while Mussolini and his Fascist Party were in power. Mussolini aligned himself with the Germans, even though the Germans knew that the Italians didn't have a lot of military strength to provide for the invasion of Great Britain. In September 1943, Mussolini was forced from power, and with his fall, Italy changed sides in the war – moving from siding/fighting with the Germans, to signing an Armistice, and siding with the Allies. Germany did NOT take this switch of allegiance well and set out to destroy Italy.

Northern Italy was still a predominantly fascist area, while southern Italy moved back to being more socialist in nature.

Back home, I heard people cheering and shouting about the Armistice and declaring, "The war is over, the war is over." The war wasn't even close to being over. Montgomery and Patton may have landed in Sicily, but the war was NOT over.

In Rome, the Germans took over, and forced the Italian army to disband, effectively taking control of the capital and beginning its quest to take over all of Italy. If anyone shot a German, Germany swore (and followed through on the threat) to kill 10 civilians for each German casualty.

Grotte Ardeatine Monument – outside.

Someone in Rome shot 36 Germans in a fit of rage. In return, the Germans (controlled by the SS) gathered up 360 Italian civilians and put them in a cave. They allowed a priest to enter the cave with the civilians, in order to perform last rites, but the Germans shot everyone – including the priest. Once they were done their slaughter, the Germans closed the face of the cave and left it as a mass burial ground. That place is now the Grotte Ardeatine Monument.

Grotte Ardeatine Monument – crypts inside for all of the victims.

Rationing started to have an effect in Ferentino. It was time to slaughter the pig and we didn't have any salt. I'm not sure how, but we found out that there was salt available in a town 15-20 miles to the south (towards the front), and one guy from town went down to pick up enough salt for everyone.

Remember where we lived...down a cart-path from the main road. When the salt arrived, my brother and I were sent to the road to get our family's share – a 20-pound sack and a 30-pound sack. We had to drag those bags of salt the three miles down the path to the house. We didn't care, we had salt to slaughter the pig. That was what counted.

By now, it wasn't unusual to have Germans around the neighborhood. They were getting bolder and nastier, and seemed to be everywhere.

In November of 1943, four SS troopers, black boots, sunglasses and all, showed up at our door. My aunt, Vittoria (Luigi's wife), was baking bread at the back of the house, and my mother was helping. The SS trooper came upon me first. "Where is your father?", he asked. I answered, truthfully, "In America." That earned me a slap across the mouth. These were NOT nice people. When they asked where my mother was, I said she was out back baking bread.

Remember, by this time, our house had grown to three stories. It was the biggest house in the area. The size and location – near the paper factory – made it very desirable for the Germans.

The kitchen where the bread was made – this was behind the store.

The oven where we made bread.

Uncle Luigi's family

The tenants (who worked at the paper factory) outside of the house.

My uncle came out, and the SS troopers ordered us to leave our home – all of us – in an hour. He gave us one hour to get out and take everything with us. They needed the space for barracks for the soldiers. As we were preparing to leave, we watched tanks coming down our path...the path that ended at the paper factory.

We didn't have many possessions, but we did have food – and that food needed to be protected and preserved, so that we wouldn't starve.

Everyone grabbed what they could. Those things that we couldn't grab were thrown out the window and scavenged by refugees coming through from the south. We all moved about a mile away, into a cousin's kitchen. The houses just got more crowded than they already were. The SS was now living in our house because it was large, and worked well as a barracks.

The Germans also brought their tanks, six or eight of them, down the cart path from the main road that ended at the paper factory, in front of Luigi's store (our house). Once the tanks got there, they got stuck. The only way to leave was to turn around and go back the way they had come – back to the main road – back TOWARDS the front. Not a good move on their part!

From September 1943 – January 1944, we saw refugees from Monte Cassino (49 miles to the south) every day. They came by begging for food. Twenty-five thousand refugees were fleeing the Germans, and heading north. Fear and hunger are powerful forces, and we didn't have any extra food to share.

To protect the stash, Mom dug a hole in the floor of the storage area at my cousin's, where we hid all the food. We would uncover the secret hole in the morning, remove all the items that we needed for the day, then cover the hole back up.

My cousin's house (as it was in 1995) where we lived in the kitchen while our house was occupied by the Germans.

The bombings were coming closer to us and more often. The men got together and dug a shelter in the hill by the creek next to where we used to gather our water. The earth was sort of like a clay, so they could dig a 'cave' in the side of the hill. They made it a "U" shape – never wanting only one exit in case of attack. Along the "U", there were alcoves dug off of the main tunnel – one in which each family could sleep. Just outside of the "entrances" to the cave was a spring that we went to for the drinking water.

We didn't need to use the cave until the front lines broke through Monte Cassino and moved from where they'd fought for 123 days, when the Germans started moving north – towards Ferentino. The Allies broke through the front lines in Monte Cassino in May of 1944. Nothing was left of that town. All the civilians had fled. Each night, the Allies or the Germans would wave a white flag, go into the field of battle and retrieve their dead, then go back to fighting the next day. The Allies - the Americans, English and Polish, lost over 50,000 men.

Amazingly enough, I wasn't afraid…believe it or not, you get used to the fighting…you get used to the war.

The war was raging on our land in May of 1944.

Ferentino after the bombings – May 24, 1944.

As the Allies began to close in on Ferentino, the Germans decided to move their tanks out – to make an escape and save the equipment – and to try to head north to Anzio and Nettuno. The Nazis left our land and started heading back down the cart path towards the main road (because it was the only way out) only to run right into the Allies. Two or three of the tanks were bombed as the Germans tried to escape.

There is a certain satisfaction (not that you want to see anyone die) in seeing the SS guys who kicked you out of your house get shot by the Allied troops. The deceased SS men were buried in the fields around our houses, and not surprisingly, the corn and wheat grew very high around the burial sites. They provided extra fertilizer. We never took that for granted in the years to come.

Leandro and me outside of the shelter in 1995.

My grandkids - Michelle, Mike's daughter; Drew, Andy's son; and me.

We moved into the shelter of the cave in May 1944. There were seven or eight families in this cave. Probably 20 or 30 people.

We would play in and around the shelter during the day, and sleep in the cave at night. We had brought as much food as we could, but it didn't last. This was the first time that I ever remember being really hungry.

Above the cave, on top of the hill, grew a beautiful cherry tree. Larry, my friend (who was also staying in the cave with his family), and I would climb the hill, then climb the tree, and eat ourselves sick on cherries. We'd eat them pit and all...as many as we could pick. It helped to curb the hunger.

Keep in mind, the war was all around us. Bombs were constantly exploding. You could hear gunfire all around.

One day, as Larry and I were up in the cherry tree, an artillery shell came screaming in. It hit near the base of the cherry tree that we were in, and should have exploded – but it didn't. Somehow, the shell hit near the base of the tree, then skipped away (that's the only word I can use, it literally skipped off of the ground) from the tree and exploded – a little way away from the cherry tree.

Larry and I jumped from the tree and down into the cave faster than you can say 'boom'! I don't think that we ventured far from the cave for quite a while.

We lived in the cave for three weeks or a month...until the fighting had moved past our land.

My mother and I were still living in my cousin's kitchen when the Allies came through in June. The Allies realized that their tanks were too big to take through Ferentino, so they built a 'by-pass' to the south of the town of Ferentino along which they could move the tanks and the "mechanical army". So, while the machinery moved along the road outside of Ferentino, the countryside still needed to be cleared by foot soldiers because no tanks/jeeps could cross the rough countryside. As an aside, since that time, a new turnpike was put up across the countryside – in fact, the turnpike runs right through where my cousin's house used to be.

When the Americans got to Ferentino, they set up their camp close to where we were living. I got to be friends with some of them...sort of a mascot, probably. They would let me go through the chow line with them. For the first time in my life, I tasted canned fruit, peaches and pears. Before that time, I had only ever had fresh fruit.

One night, one of the guys was done eating and decided that he needed to clean his teeth. He pushed them out of his mouth – both top and bottom – with the flick of a tongue! What the heck?!?! I thought he'd shot his teeth out of his mouth to bite me! He got a good laugh at my reaction...I had never seen dentures before. Quite frankly, it scared the hell out of me!

I also got my first taste of chewing gum. As one of the troop trains was going by on the railroad, one serviceman threw a pack of Chicklets out the window to me. I picked it up and started chewing it. I thought it was a sugar candy, but when I got to the gum itself, I spat it out! What the heck is this? I thought it was a joke.

The Americans, British and French were the primary Allies that were in Italy. The French Army employed a large number of Moroccan "volunteers" as foot soldiers.

While the "mechanized army" moved along the by-pass around Ferentino, the "foot army" (comprised mostly of Moroccans, and commanded by the British) were the ones who came through the land surrounding Ferentino – including through our neighborhood.

Unfortunately, while the British "commanded" the Moroccans, they couldn't really "control" them. The Moroccans began raping the women they came across as they made their way through the countryside. When the local men approached the British Commanders for help, the Brits said that they had no control over the Moroccans, that they were just stuck with them.

"Please stop them," said the locals.
"We can't," said the British, "but it's OK if you kill them. We'll clean up the mess."

They literally told us that it was OK if we killed the Moroccans who were raping the women. There would be no problems if we did. So, the civilians of Ferentino started an entirely new war – this time with the Moroccans.

My mother was 44 at the time. I saw her, Leandro's wife and her sister, and my cousin's wife jump out of windows of their houses three or four different times to escape the unwanted attention of a Moroccan foot soldier.

Now, we'd scavenged a lot of guns and ammunition from the Germans when they were killed, from when they abandoned them as they left. We were armed. We shot the Moroccans. We lost one local man, but the Moroccans lost a lot of their comrades. The British helped us "clean up" after them and buried the Moroccans in an area of the family property that was to become a gravel pit.

After the Germans left, we found a case of dynamite. The dynamite was a little cube (3" x 3" x 3") with a little hole in the top that had a cap and a fuse inside. Light the fuse, it would burn down inside the cube and detonate. We'd light the dynamite and throw it into the pond by the factory. It would blow up and kill all the fish in the area of the explosion in the water. The dead fish would float to the top of the water, and we'd pick them out. For a few weeks, we ate REALLY well – fish every night for dinner!

Uncle Luigi at one of the gravel pits in 1995.

When the British moved on, they left us provisions. They left us food. They left us ammunition. They treated us well.

We moved back into our house above the dry-goods store in July of 1944. Soldiers were still coming through, but everything was OK. The killing and devastation had stopped.

By the end of 1944, things were getting back to "normal" in our little corner of the world. The war had left our region. We were living in our own homes. We returned to the cycle that we'd known for so many years.

The Allied Cemetery at Netuno for Monte Cassino casualties – years later – so many gave all.

<u>AFTER THE WAR</u>

By 1945, the rest of the world started to stabilize. Letters began to flow between Italy and the United States. My father decided to bring Americo to the States. Again, my father didn't seem to want the entire family. He could have brought Mom, Americo and me (Leandro was on his own by then) to the U.S. Instead, Americo set off on October 9, 1946 on his "adventure" – alone – on a ship called the Marine Perch. When Americo got to New York, he began working at a deli and fruit stand at 36th Street and 9th Avenue in Manhattan.

Peter, my dad, in New York in 1945 with my cousin (my uncle's daughter) and her family.

For me, well, my father didn't send for me. Instead, he sent me shoes. My first pair of new shoes – ever – and they were too small. I was so upset. I had to give them away. Most of the time, I went barefoot – summer and winter!

When September 1946 came, and the schools in the area restarted. My mother sent me to fifth grade in the town of Ferentino – five miles away. I didn't do well in this new school. School went from 9 a.m. to 1 p.m. I had to walk five miles there, down a dirt path, and five miles back (I begged my mother to let me take the bus, but the walk to the bus stop was two and a half miles in the opposite direction, then waiting for the bus. I really wouldn't have gained any time – even if we had had the bus fare – which we didn't). The school loaded us up with homework, but by the time I got home, it was dark. We didn't have lights, so I couldn't do the work. By June 1947, I had flunked out of fifth grade.

My father came home for a visit in July of 1947 (he left New York June 26th for Italy according to the ship's manifest).

When he got there and found out I'd flunked, he threw up his hands and said, "What are we going to do with this boy?"

He decided that I would go to the seminary in Rome in the fall of 1947. For only the second time in my life, I was spending nights away from my home.

The Collegio Apostolico Leoniano <u>Seminary</u> was at the end of the Via Germonico on the far-side of the piazza (circle).

One of the buildings in the seminary (as it looks today).

We had a chapel at the base of the hill to Ferentino that we attended when we could make the 4 ½ mile walk, but I'd never seen anything like the structure of the school or church services in the Seminary. I had grown up with a lot of freedom. Being in the seminary was like being in jail. We had to go to church in the seminary five to seven times a day. We'd start by praying the Rosary at 5 a.m. up on the roof. From there, we'd go to breakfast, then back to Church, on to school, back to church, lunch, church again, school, homework, then church again. This was NOT fun for me!

I became an alter server. The church we served? St. Peter's Cathedral – The Pope's "Church"!!! There were a bunch of chapels in the Cathedral, and services going almost non-stop, so there was always a need for altar servers. Since we lived at the seminary, we were always available to do our duty. They would march us down the street from the seminary to St. Peter's (which had 24 alters) two-by-two.

Me in the seminary – I'm peaking out from the top-left corner.

My godparents lived down the street from the seminary, and sometimes they'd stop by to see me. My cousins (Roseanna, Rita and Roberta) would see us as we were walking to St. Peter's.

They would snicker at me and taunt me as we passed – part of the little army going to serve the Lord.

At home, our meals were simple, but good, and we always had plenty to eat. The food in the seminary was lousy, simply lousy. We were constantly served bean soup. The beans were actually rotted and had bugs, complete with wings, in them. I would pull the bugs out of the soup and line them up on the side of the bowl. After a while, I just couldn't eat it any more.

The dining hall at the seminary had a long table with boys sitting on either side. About halfway down the table, someone would read from the Bible to "entertain" us during the meals. At the front of the dining hall, up on a pedestal, sat the Rector, watching over his "charges".

One day, the Rector noticed that I wasn't eating.

"Cocco, eat your soup!"

I replied, "I can't eat all these flies."

"Would you like to trade?" he asked.

"Yes, thank you," I answered.

He was SHOCKED! He was shocked, but he did trade with me because he had offered. Imagine my surprise when I found out that he had delicious chicken soup! None of the rotten bean soup that the students had. I thoroughly enjoyed that meal. Needless to say, he never asked anyone if they wanted to switch again.

Leandro would come to visit me and smuggle in sausage and bread. The priests wondered why I wasn't eating. Someone ratted me out, and they took away my stash. It was back to the rotten bean soup.

Occasionally, we'd be marched (yes, marched) down the street a couple of miles to a soccer field, so that we could play for a while.

By December 1947, I had had it with the seminary. When

Leandro came to visit me, I told him that I was going to the United States. "I am an American citizen, so I am going to the U.S. Either you help me get there, or I will run away and figure it out for myself."

Remember, my father was a U.S. citizen before I was born, so I was a U.S. citizen.

"Where will you go?" asked Leandro.

"I'll stay with my brother." (Americo was already in America).

"Finish the year out at the Seminary, then we'll work it out."

"I'm not going to make it. No, I'm leaving."

This discussion went on for a few months, but by the beginning of April 1948, I said that if he didn't get me out, I was going to leave and run. He had a choice, help me or don't help me, but I was done. D-o-n-e. Done.

THE JOURNEY TO AMERICA

Apparently, while I was making my case to Leandro about going to the U.S., when he came to visit me at the seminary, my mother was making her own demands of my father. My father had "made a motion" to take me to America, but my mother wasn't having any of that story. Her demand was simple – "You're not leaving without me. All three of us go to America." They had been separated for 27 years of their married life, and she was done with being apart.

My father finally agreed – he'd take both of us, my mother, Barbara and me, with him to the United States.

Leandro wasn't coming with us because by this time he'd married. He and his wife moved into our old house on the third floor when we left for America.

After what seemed like useless and endless delays, May came and we left Ferentino for Naples where we would get a ship to the

United States.

Leandro and his wife took us down to Naples by bus. We carried all of our worldly possessions, which was not very much, in one steamer trunk.

I had my second "eye opening" experience, another "WOW" moment like when I went to Rome, when we arrived in Naples. I saw the huge ships, the cars, the trucks, the people, the cranes. I'd never seen a crane. I watched in amazement as they would pick up the huge steamer trunks and deposit them on the deck of the ship.

The ship that would take us to America was the Vulcania. We sailed on May 5, 1948.

The Vulcania – "My" Ship

As soon as we went on board the ship, I ran to the bow just to absorb everything that was going on. It was a great view! I saw Leandro and my sister-in-law down on the dock, and we waved. We were all crying a little bit because we didn't know if we'd ever see each other again. I heard massive horns sounding, lines being thrown off, tugboats pushing, and we began moving. We were on our way!

I watched the city of Naples grow smaller, and Mount Vesuvius dwindle. The tears started to flow. I never thought I'd see Italy again, and it was my home. As excited as I was to go to America, the finality of leaving Italy struck me as we pulled out of the harbor, and I got a little scared.

I stayed on the bow until I couldn't see land any more. Finally, I went below deck and found my mother down in the third class area. Third class was divided into two sections – women/children and men. The groups were separated during the long voyage, but would come together in the dining hall to eat.

Our first day at sea an announcement came over the loudspeaker: "We need altar servers. They hadn't even finished the announcement, and I was on my way to volunteer. I served mass every day of the voyage up in second class, so I got to see how the "better class" lived. I even snuck a peek into first class on occasion. They had lounge chairs and lovely deck areas – very different than down in the dismal third class quarters. You couldn't even sneak into first class because it was gated.

Down in third class, the smell was awful. My mother was sick for most of the trip – probably due to the smells and cramped conditions. I was on a top bunk (I wasn't old enough to be on the 'men's side'), and my mother was on the bottom bunk.

I spent my time up during the trip on the deck, watching and dreaming. I saw fish swimming with the ship and figured they were looking for food. When I finally mentioned it to someone, they said "No, those aren't fish, they are dolphins and they are escorting the ship." They stayed with us for a while.

The journey itself was uneventful...no stories of crashing waves or anything.

After what seemed like forever, but was really 10 days, I began to see changes on the horizon as I watched from the bow. I saw a herd of sheep on the shoreline...a large herd of sheep...the largest herd of sheep I'd ever seen. I got my father and told him to look at all the sheep. "Those aren't sheep, Enzo, those are cars on West River Drive." Imagine my surprise! That many cars in one place. Amazing.

My father gave me three quarters before we arrived in America. "You can go to three movies – one with each quarter." I had seen one movie in my life, maybe, when I was in Rome with my eye! Oh, the changes that were in store for me.

We passed the Statue of Liberty and were processed through Ellis Island. While my father and I were both American citizens, my mother was not, so we had to go through Ellis Island. From Ellis Island, we took the ferry across to Manhattan.

The ferry dropped us in New York City – at 11th Avenue. We took a cab (with our trunk strapped to the back) two blocks to 406 West 36th Street (near 9th Avenue). We were at our apartment.

I arrived in the United States the same week that Israel gained its independence (Israel became independent May 14th).

The apartment was small. There was a living room, kitchen and bedroom. Through the 'big' bedroom was a very small second bedroom, only large enough for a single mattress. That was my room. Americo slept in the living room.

There was running water in the kitchen, but there were no bathrooms in the apartment. Each floor consisted of four apartments. In the hall was the toilet – with two commodes to serve the entire floor. There were no sinks in the hall – you washed your hands back in the kitchen.

The kitchen also had a coal stove. Each apartment had its own coal bin in the basement, so when my mother needed more coal, Americo or I would have to run down to the basement and haul some back up to the apartment.

Outside the kitchen window was a pulley and a laundry line. My mother would do the wash in the apartment, then hang it to dry out the window. On wash day, you'd see all the women pulling laundry in/out through their kitchen windows.

To get a bath, you had to go to 39th or 40th streets, to a public bathhouse. For a dime, you would get a shower – with hot and cold running water (amazing to me) – and a towel! I thought that was a great deal.

My mother and me in our apartment soon after we'd arrived in America.

I didn't know it then, but the area we lived in was called "Hell's Kitchen". It was a land of tenements. I don't know why it was called that, but I guess because it was hell to live there. To me, it was a step up in the world. We had running water inside, and a bathroom, and electricity.

In the days that followed our arrival in New York, I walked all over the neighborhoods around our apartment. Of course, I was wearing the short pants that I wore my whole life in Italy. I noticed a lot of people giving me odd looks. I turned to my father for advice.

Me in 1948 – My first "official" portrait.

"Papà, why are they looking at me like that?"

Of course, I didn't know that kids my age didn't wear short pants in New York. Dad looked me up and down, then decided that a change was in order. He took me out to the store and bought me two pairs of long pants. With that simple change, the odd looks stopped.

Dad also got me to join the club at the Police Athletic League (PAL) at 9th Avenue and 38th Street. They had all kinds of things for kids to do – pool, ping pong, basketball. Just everything! Unfortunately, I couldn't play because I didn't understand ANYTHING that anyone said, so I went to my father again.

"Papà, I don't understand anything."

"You'll be OK."

That was his entire commentary, "You'll be OK."

I went to the movies (which were in English) with my three quarters.

I went to the PAL. I listened. I learned.

Finally, I felt confident enough in my English to say "Excuse me, may I have the next game" to the guys at the pool table at the PAL club. They laughed and said, "Listen to the Little Guinea," but they let me into the game.

I learned. I learned fast.

I came to New York City as 'Enzo'. There was a girl called Ramona, who was NOT Italian, who lived in our tenement (actually, on our floor), and was about my age. I kind of liked her (remember, I'm about 15 by now), so I asked her if she wanted to go to the movies. She said, 'yes', so we went out a couple of times, but it didn't really 'take'.

Ramona would call me 'Anzu'. I asked her, "Why do you call me 'Anzu', my name is 'Enzo', I don't like 'Anzu'."

"Fine," she said, "in that case, I'll call you 'Andy'."

"What is 'Andy'?" I asked.

"A diminutive of 'Andrew'," she replied.

"Andrew, Andy...I like it."

MY FIRST PAYING JOB

I spent my three quarters at the movies at the Chelsea Movie Theater on 9th Avenue. I went back to my father and asked for another 25¢, so that I could see another movie. My father walked over to the front of the living room and out onto the fire escape.

"Come here, Enzo," he called. "What do you see out there?"

"I don't see anything but people and trucks and cars. I see a factory down the street. I see dust, and the entrance to the Lincoln Tunnel."

"There's a lot of money out there...why don't you go out and get your own."

I said, "How do I do that?"

He said, "Just go out there and you'll find out. Go take a walk."

I left the apartment and went walking. I walked all over the area around my house. I saw kids on some of the street corners around 34th Street shining shoes. I said to myself, "I can do that."

I went back to the apartment to talk to my father.

"Papà, can you lend me $5.00?"

My father never said a word. He simply opened his wallet, took out $5.00 and gave it to me. He never asked me a question. He never asked me what I was going to do with it. He just gave it to me.

I took the $5.00 and went back out to purchase a shoe-shine box. I'd already checked out the store where you could buy them, so I knew that $5.00 would cover the cost and leave me a few pennies to spare. I bought the box, brown and black polish, brushes, the whole shebang.

I left the store and went looking for the perfect spot to 'open shop'. I found it at 34th Street and 8th Avenue – right across the street from the New Yorker Hotel (where the Yankees used to stay when they were playing in the Bronx).

"My" corner was the southwest corner. Penn Station (the train station) was at 33rd Street. The main Post Office was on 8th Avenue between 31st and 33rd streets. I was right in the heart of the action!

New Yorker Hotel

I put my box down and was in business. About 20 minutes later, a guy stopped and asked me how much. I answered, "No speak English." He puts his foot up anyway, and I shined his shoes. When I was done, he gave me 25¢. I'd earned my first money! It felt great!

Rather than carting the shoeshine box home at night, I looked for a place to store it. I went down in the subway station. For 10¢, I could rent a locker for 24 hours. I'd put the shoeshine box in the locker, pocket the key, then head home, and pick it up again in the morning.

Back in those days, there was a newsstand on almost every corner where there was a subway entrance. At "my" intersection, there were three newsstands. I got to know the guys who ran them. They were kind to me. They gave me advice.

For four days, everything was great. On the fifth day, a police car kept driving by me and my corner. The cop kept waving at me out the window and hollering to me, but I didn't understand what he was saying. I waved back. I thought he was being friendly.

After a little while, the police car came by again, stopped, and walked over to me. Again, the cops said something that I didn't understand. Then, they took my shoeshine box, locked it in the trunk of their car, and drove away. They just took it! I had no idea why.

When I went to one of the newsstand vendor and told him what happened, he told me that there are shoeshine people who make a living shining shoes, and you can't just take over their business. It's OK to stay on a corner a little while, the cops will overlook that, but you can't stay there all day, every day. You have to move around.

At that point, I just wanted to know how to get my shoeshine box back!

"Well," said the newsstand vendor, "Go to the police station and ask for it back."

"Where is that?"

He directed me a few blocks away...something like 28th Street...and off I went.

When I got to the police station, I couldn't get anyone to understand what I wanted, but there was a cop who spoke Italian. I explained that I was just trying to get my shoeshine box back and couldn't understand why they'd taken it.

"Ah...come with me. We don't mind you shining shoes on the corner, but when we wave you off, you've got to move."

He took me downstairs, down in the basement of the precinct, and he unlocked a door. When he opened it up, there was a huge room just FILLED with shoeshine boxes. Everywhere you looked, there were shoeshine boxes in all shapes and sizes. I wasn't the first person that this had happened to!

"Do you see yours?" asked the man.

I decided to put my ingenuity to work. I saw a really nice box – one where you could sit on it, and flip it open to get to the footrest – in the pile.

"Yes, it's that one right there," I answered. Of course, I was pointing to that nice shoeshine box!

"Did you have a chair?" he proceeds to ask.

"Yes, that one," I responded.

I walked out of that police station with a better shoeshine box AND a chair! Of course, I headed right back to "my" corner.

Shortly after I returned, the same police car drove by. When they saw me back – and with a bigger/better shoeshine box – their expressions said, "What the heck?" I didn't wait for them to come by again...I cleared out right away.

Now that I had this nice gear, I decided to put the price for a shine on a sign on the side of my box. 15¢. Very professional looking. I was very proud of that sign. After a few shines where I got only 15¢ (as opposed to 20¢ or 25¢), I decided to take the sign down, and go back to my "No speak English" response when they asked me, "How much?" I made a lot more when I didn't have my price listed anywhere!

I shined shoes for about five months. I also tried delivering groceries on the Upper West Side (north of Columbus Circle, up by Central Park), but there wasn't any money in it, so I only lasted four days and went back to shining shoes.

For a couple of months while I was shining shoes, I also worked for a horse handicapper. This guy would put the names of the horses in envelopes, then sell the envelopes for $2.00/envelope. The guy would give me a stack of envelopes, bundled together by subway stop. I'd take the train out to the last stop in Brooklyn, then I'd work my way back to Manhattan, getting off at every subway stop along the way. At each stop, I'd run up to the street to the newsstand, and drop off their package of envelopes. Then, I'd run back into the subway (the guy who hired me paid my subway fares) and catch the next train. I'd get off at the next stop and repeat the process. Eventually, I ended up in Times Square which was the end of my 'route'.

Apparently, there was some "trouble" with the law because one day the guy who hired me to run these envelopes said, "We'd better stop for a while, Kid." That was the end of that for my 'gambling' work.

One day in July, my father and I were walking along 9th Avenue, maybe six or seven blocks from our apartment (probably 28th or 30th streets), and we saw a trailer parked along the street with a loudspeaker inviting you to come in for 'Free X-Rays'.

"What do they mean, Papà? I want to see what this is."

"It's nothing you'd be interested in," said my father. "It's a picture of your bones."

I dragged my father in the door. There were two doors to the thing – one to enter, one to exit, and a picture in the middle. So, we had our "pictures" taken. About a week later, someone from the Board of Health came to the house. The x-rays of my father's chest showed tuberculosis, and they took him away to Bellevue Hospital. My dad spent the next six months in that hospital. My curiosity probably saved his life!

When they took dad, the Health Department also checked both Mom and me out. We checked out OK.

Luckily, I was making more money than we needed to live, so we were OK while Dad was in the hospital.

SCHOOL

In September 1948, my parents enrolled me in PS11 on West 21st Street.

No one knew what grade to put me in, but they did have a special teacher to help immigrant kids. We'd go to a class to learn English for two periods each day. They taught us how to speak the language. First, they'd teach us the word, then they'd teach us how to use the word in a sentence. For example, the word "glass". The teacher would hold up a glass and say, "glass." Then the teacher would say, "The glass is empty." You could learn pretty quickly this way.

I enjoyed math. Numbers are the same in any language. I didn't like the other classes too much.

PS11 as it stands in 2016...we didn't have the air conditioners back in 1948!

At some point, the principal started singing Italian songs to me. I didn't respond to him because I didn't know the songs. Finally, the principal asked someone, "What's wrong with him?" They asked me, and I answered, "I don't have a radio...I don't know those songs."

We had a cage on the roof of the school where we used to go and play softball. I enjoyed sports, and enjoyed playing. We played other schools and must have been pretty good because we won a trophy. In 1949, Roy Campanella and Jackie Robinson (who both played for the Brooklyn Dodgers) came to the school to present our softball team with the trophy! Oh, I wish I had a photograph of that.

Roy Campanella and Jackie Robinson in the dugout.

I loved taking the subway up to the Bronx to watch the Yankees play in the old Yankee Stadium. In 1948/1949, you could get a bleacher seat for 25¢!

I'd go to school until about 2 p.m., then I'd go off to work. I loved math and learning English, but I wasn't interested in any of the other lessons. Because my English was so bad, I only had to go to my English class and my math classes. I advanced in both of those. I went to PS11 for two years (until June 1950).

MOVING UP IN THE WORLD

By the time fall came and I'd started school, the most profitable of the three newsstand owners at "my" corner had taken a liking to me. He was a nice, Jewish guy who had a big house in Long Island, and a swimming pool. After I'd been on "my" corner a few months, he knew that my dad was in the hospital with tuberculosis. "I'm sorry, kid. That's tough." Then, he said to me, "I'm going to get you a job with the papers." At the time, there were a bunch of morning papers and five, count 'em five, evening papers. Most papers printed twice a day – morning and evening. In the evening, there was the Times, the Post, the Journal American, the Star Telegraph, and the Herald.

Somehow, the newspapers had to get from where they were printed (they were all printed in Manhattan back then) to the newsstands where they were sold. The trucks bringing the papers from the printing presses dropped bundles every so often...not at every newsstand. The papers then paid a guy to wait at certain "stations" for the papers to be dropped from the truck. When the papers hit the ground, that guy would break apart the large bundles, and put them in smaller bunches of papers. When he'd gotten them all organized, he would deliver them to all of the newsstands on his route. I became "that guy".

I got hired as the delivery boy for the area around the New York Times building (Times Square). When I went to the Social Security office to apply for a Social Security Number, I applied as "Andrew Enzo Cocco". From that moment on, I was Andrew Cocco! It became official. Ever since then, I've been "Andy".

A typical newsstand in the 1940s...this one wasn't mine.

Every evening, I'd wait outside the New York Times building
(which was at 1 Times Square) for the papers to be dropped from
the truck. I'd cut the bundles using a hook that looped around
my finger and had a razor affixed (a ring with a razor blade
attached). It was a special 'tool' that we used. I would 'rip, strip,
and flip' the papers (open the bundles, count off the papers for
each newsstand, and pile for delivery)! That meant that I divided
them up into the bundles that would be dropped at each of the
newsstands (so many of paper 1, so many of paper 2, etc. for each
stand). Once that was done, I'd deliver the papers to each of the
newsstands in my 'territory'.

The New York Times Building – 1 Times Square (behind the Pepsi-Cola sign).

For that work, I received the princely sum of $12 per paper per week. I was earning $60 per week! This was a FORTUNE to me. My dad was making $2.00/hour as a rock-driller before he got sick. Imagine, I was making more money than my father!

On one of the corners was a jewelry store next to a Nedick's. In front of the jewelry store there was a newsstand run by disabled war veterans. These guys let me sell two late, late papers (those that came after the evening editions) – the *News* and the *Mirror* – after I delivered my other papers. Those papers sold for the princely sum of 3¢ per paper! When the weather was bad, the vets weren't able to sit out in the rain/cold to sell papers at all, so they'd let me take over for the day. The jeweler was a kind man who would leave the awning down, even after he closed, so that the papers and I would stay dry. The vets let me keep all of the profit for what I sold. If you didn't sell all your papers, technically, you had to cover the cost of the ones you didn't sell, but they'd take back the unsold papers, so I got to keep my whole profit.

Those days, when I was actually selling the papers, I was the

'Extra. Extra. Read all about it.' kid! That's where I really learned English.

Nedick's was known for its orange drink.

A typical Nedick's shop on a corner in Manhattan.

At "my" corner, there was also a Nedick's coffee shop. Nedick's sold coffee, hotdogs and pie, among other things. At the end of the night, if there was leftover pie, the owner would give it to me to take home.

With the first "real" money I made, I bought a pair of roller skates. I went everywhere on those skates.

About this time, Americo left his job with the deli and fruit stand and went to work for the Good Humor Company in Brooklyn. The best part of that was that we always had sweet treats!

DAD LEAVES THE HOSPITAL

Dad got out of the hospital in 1949. While he was gone, we'd received a notice that the tenement in which we lived was being torn down to make way for future development. We had to leave, but we had some time before we had to skedaddle.

About this time, I found out that they were building the first Levittown out on Long Island.

Levittown was the first planned community, built of modest houses that many people could afford.

These little Cape Cod bungalows had 1 ½ baths and a kitchen, plus several bedrooms – all for $10,000. Imagine having 1 ½ baths right in your home? I tried to talk my dad into allowing me to buy one for us. My father wouldn't hear of it. He didn't want his 17-year-old supporting HIM.

"I can afford it," I said.

"No you can't. I never went to school here," he said, "but if I had learned English I wouldn't be as sick as I am now, because I would've had a better job than being a rock driller, breathing all that dust. I'm not going to let you buy a Levittown house. You're going to learn English, lose your accent (don't speak to anyone from Italy) and move up in the world. If I hear you speaking Italian, I'm going to kick your butt!"

We didn't buy the house, but we still had to get out of the tenement.

THE MOVE TO PHILADELPHIA

In July or August of 1950, friends from Italy, the Palumbos, who lived in Philadelphia, came to visit us in New York. They wanted us to move down there, claiming the cost of living was lower, and that Dad could live better on his pension. Dad took a trip down to check things out and he liked what he saw. It was time to move.

We bought our first house at 244 North Felton Street in West Philadelphia (the Overbrook area as its known now). The house was built in 1925, so it was relatively new and nice. It was a converted row house with an apartment upstairs. The downstairs had three rooms; a bedroom, a bathroom and a living room.

We rented out the second floor and lived on the first floor. Each floor had its own bath, so it was quite luxurious. We also had a little backyard.

I fought the move tooth and nail. I didn't want to move with my parents. I'd started making a life in New York. So, when my parents moved to Philly, I stayed behind. That lasted maybe three months, so by the end of August 1950, I'd moved to Philadelphia, as well.

244 North Felton Street, Philadelphia.

In Philly, I had a bedroom all to myself because Americo had been drafted before we moved.

The newspaper business in Philly was dead. Therefore, I thought that Philly was dead. Regardless, I had to figure out some other way to earn money.

When I asked my dad about the opportunities in the area, again he said, "lose the accent."

MY FIRST JOBS AND SCHOOL IN PHILLY

First, I enrolled at Dobbins Vocational School at 21st and Lehigh across the street from Shibe Park (the home of the Philadelphia A's and the Philadelphia Phillies). I signed up for the auto mechanic and body & fender classes. They also had classes for immigrants to learn English, so I signed up for those, as well.

I still needed a job, so I went out and wandered down 63rd Street to see what was around.

I saw a bowling alley and went inside to see what was what. The first thing that I saw were the 'duck pins' (smaller-than-normal bowling pins), which were knocked down with a small ball (like a bocce ball) that you held in your hand. I asked the guy, Murphy, to explain it to me, and he suggested I try a game or two. The cost was 25 or 30¢ a game, so I bowled a couple of games. Turns out, I was pretty good at it because it was a lot like bocce that we used to play in Italy. Murphy said, "You're pretty good. Why don't you try regular bowling?" So I did. I was pretty good at that, too, so the bowling alley became my new hangout.

In fact, my father thought that this might be a bad influence for me. I finally took him to the bowling alley one day, so he could meet the guys that I had met there, and he was finally satisfied.

However, this was COSTING me money, not MAKING me money, so I had to keep looking for a way to make some income.

Right across the street from the bowling alley was an Esso station (Esso was the precursor to Exxon). Back in those days, gas stations were full-service. They filled the car, checked the oil and water under the hood, and cleaned the windows – all for the price of a tank of gas. Most gas stations also serviced the cars, doing oil changes, changing tires, etc.

I went across the street to the Esso station and saw a guy, a white-haired guy, pumping gas and working on the cars in the service bay. I went up to him and said, "I saw you pumping the gas and working on the cars. You have nice, white hair. Maybe you need some help."

The guy, whose name was Lou Kelly, said "You sound like Desi Arnez." I answered back, "I'm Italian." (FYI, Desi Arnez was Cuban). Lou hired me on the spot, and I worked for him for a few bucks.

Up the street, at 63rd and Haverford, there was a Sunoco station. I went up to that station and got a job there, as well. Gas was 22¢ a gallon at the time. I pumped the gas, greased the cars (they needed to be greased every 1,000 miles), added oil, and checked the fluids. In the winter, I put chains on the cars, so they could get around in the snow, for $2.00 per set.

I sort of went gas station to gas station, picking up hours wherever I could when I wasn't in school learning to be an auto mechanic.

After a while, I found Merit Mercury in Landsdowne, Pa. Merit Mercury was a car dealership with a gas station a block away. The gas station also did the servicing of the cars for the dealership.

So, I'm going to school at Dobbins during the day to be an auto mechanic, and I'm working at Merit Mercury on nights and weekends. I decide that if I'm going to be in the car business, I'd better get a car! I bought an old junker, an old '41 Ford, and had it towed and parked it behind the station. Slowly, on my own time, I restored the thing.

My English was improving, but it wasn't great yet. One day, a sailor pulled into the station, jumps out of the car and says, "Where's your head?"

Me as a mechanic.

The rebuilt car – I was the only one of my friends with a convertible! Sara is on the left. Miranda, on the right, was in our wedding.

Well, I wasn't going to fall for that one! I was NOT going to point to my head, so I stayed silent. I was not going to answer.

"What's wrong with you? Where's your head?"

Still I don't answer.

"C'mon, buddy. I've gotta pee!"

AHA!!! I pointed him right to the bathroom.

I became the night manager at Merit Mercury. I was 18 or 19 years-old, and I had a pretty good job. Life was starting to fall into place.

DATING AND SARA

When I was working at the Sunoco station, I worked with a guy who had a sister, Mary Ann. I kinda liked the look of her. I asked the guy if she might go on a date, to a movie or the Hot Shop (a drive-in with waitresses on roller skates) with me. He checked and came back with, "No, she's not going to go out with a Guinea."

So, I tried another girl, and she accepted. When I picked her up, she said, "Let's play a little game. Every time a car comes by with only one headlight, we'll slap each other." Well, I thought that was really weird, but I agreed. We saw the first car with one headlight burned out (the headlights didn't last long back then), and she slapped me. We saw another one and she slapped me harder. We saw a third one and she really slapped me. Well, I'd had enough of this. The next one we see coming, well, I get ready. As it approached, I threw out my hand and back-handed her across the cheek – hard.

The next thing she says is, "We're going home." Fine by me. That was the end of that.

I was living in an Irish neighborhood, but as we all know, I'm Italian. Back in those days, the Irish and Italians didn't really 'mix'. When my family went to the church up the street to register, the church, which was Irish, told us that we couldn't worship there...we had to go to St. Donato (the Italian church) a couple of blocks away (405 North 65th Street). That's where we joined.

St. Donato's used to have dances, and I liked to go.

Luckily, I did because it was at one of those dances that I met my wife, Sara. If you ask Sara, she will tell you that we met at a picnic. Maybe we did, but we might only have exchanged a couple of words like "How do you do?", but I guess that was enough and she fell head over heels for me. You know how that is! We REALLY met at a dance at the church. We started dating, and things went pretty well.

1953 was a big year for me. I was due to graduate from Dobbins in June, but the U.S. government had other plans.

In January 1953, I received my draft notice...it was time for me to report to the U.S. Army. Americo, who got drafted in 1950, had gone to Korea as a foot soldier. The Korean war was still going on in 1953, and he recommended that I NOT join the Army.

I went to the Draft Board and explained that I'd been working hard to get my education, and that I would be getting a diploma in June. It was so important for me to get that diploma. I wanted to finish it up. The Board understood and gave me a six-month deferment until I graduated.

In June 1953, I did graduate. The day I came home from graduation, I received my next draft notice. Time to report for duty. That really put a damper on my graduation excitement!

I had a choice. I could serve in the Army for two years, or I could enlist in another branch of the service for four years. The advantage to enlisting is that you wouldn't be a foot soldier. You still had to serve your country, but you might end up in a better situation.

I decided that I would enlist in the Air Force, so I went down to 401 North Broad Street in Philadelphia and signed up for four years. It only goes to figure that the Armistice was signed in July 27, 1953...I probably could have allowed myself to be drafted and serve only two years. Oh, well. Better luck next time!

Americo, after the service (he served in Korea).

AIR FORCE TRAINING

There were tears as I left my house in early July 1953 to get the subway to Philly and then the train to Upstate New York to report for basic training. Basic training was at Sampson Air Force Base (AFB) near Seneca Lake, N.Y.

Sara and I were going strong by this time. I had to leave her. I had to leave my family. It was hard. I had just graduated and was ready to start my 'real' career.

I reported for basic training. They cut my hair off, told me to 'get in line', gave me fatigues, and told me they didn't want to hear any complaints. I was smart enough to realize to keep my mouth shut. I decided to mind my own business and just do whatever I was told.

The fatigues that I was given were for someone much taller than me. I was only 5'4" tall. The crotch of the pants came down below my knees. I cut the legs off, so that they weren't too long, but I couldn't do anything with where the crotch fell, so I just kept going. I must have been a sight!

We had to run. Well, you try running with the crotch of your pants below your knees...you can't do it. When the Sergeant saw me trying to run, then saw why I couldn't run, he took it upon himself to find me pants that actually fit. He took a liking to me because I hadn't complained.

These guys (the sergeants and above) were bastards. It was their job to make your life miserable. I made sure that whatever I was assigned, I did well. There was a month, or a month and a half, where I was in charge of the latrines. For that entire time, the latrines were spotless.

I shed plenty of tears about having signed up for four years of this nonsense (particularly when I could have gotten out in two, now that the war was over).

Sara and I continued to keep in touch.

I finished up basic training in September 1953 and was assigned to Wichita Falls, Texas. We were put on a train to get from Saranac Lake, N.Y. to Texas. We stopped for a day in St. Louis and had a nice time there.

As we arrived in Wichita Falls, I encountered my first experience with segregation in the south. When we left New York, it was cool, so we were wearing our Air Force Blues. Those were our heavier uniforms. By the time we got to Texas, it was over 90 degrees, and we were sweltering. When we got off the train, we went looking for a restaurant to get a cool drink. A couple of my buddies happened to be black. When they tried to go in the door of the restaurant, they were stopped. They had to go around the back to the "colored" door. I was shocked.

The bus picked us up and took us to the barracks. We were there to learn how to be an airplane mechanic, but there were still sergeants and marching and all the things that we'd experienced at Samson AFB in New York.

Of course, I was the shortest guy. They made me the right-guide when we marched. That meant that I was the flag-bearer for our platoon. I had to follow the cadence – out in front by myself – and the platoon had to follow me!

By this time, my English was pretty good. I had a slight accent, but no one could tell what kind of an accent it was. I was really an American.

Every life has forks in the road. A wrong decision can follow you for the rest of your life.

One of the big forks in the road for me happened one hot, Sunday afternoon in the barracks. We were all hanging out, not really doing anything. One of the guys said, "We're not doing anything, why don't we take a ride and go to town?"

I responded, "What are we going to do there that we're not doing here? We don't have any money. You gonna rob a gas station?" I didn't think there was anything to be gained by going, so I stayed, but he went to town.

The next morning, that guy wasn't at Reveille (wake-up). When I asked where he was, I was told the stockade (jail). "What'd he do?" I asked. "Robbed a gas station," came the answer.

Imagine if I really HAD gone with him? My whole life would have been different because that was a fork in the road, and I would have taken the wrong branch. Something in my "gut" had told me not to go with that guy, and my "gut" had been right.

CARSWELL AFB

After six more months of training to be an airplane mechanic, sometime around March 1954, I was transferred to Carswell AFB in Fort Worth, Texas. I was finally starting my "real" Air Force career.

Me at Carswell Air Force Base, Fort Worth, Texas.

I was in the 7th Bomb Wing in the 492nd Bomb Squadron under the leadership of General Curtis LeMay. General LeMay, the cigar smoker and good drinker, was a pretty big deal. He'd had an illustrious career in the Pacific during World War II. He would have us make whiskey runs to Puerto Rico for the entire wing. One time, he even let us order what we wanted. He was a tough guy. As they say, he ran a tight ship (or plane, in this case).

Our base was a B-36 base. The B-36 planes had 10 engines each that were built by Convair in Fort Worth.

A B-36 plane can stay in the air a long time. They carry 35,000 gallons of gas and can fly from the U.S. to Africa and back without refueling.

The movie poster for *Strategic Air Command*.

The movie *Strategic Air Command* with Jimmy Stewart and June Allyson was filmed on our base while I was stationed there.

It was kind of a big deal. When I saw the movie, I laughed at how they'd made some parts of the base look, because that really wasn't how things were in "real life".

I lived on the base. If you were single, you **had** to live on the base. If you were married, you could live off the base.

As I moved from New York to Wichita Falls, Texas to Fort Worth, Texas, Sara and I kept in contact. Sara's home situation wasn't good. She was mistreated by her parents and really needed to get out.

I wanted to help her, but the pay in the service was lousy.

However, if I waited to get out of the service, find a job, save some money, then marry her...well, we'd never end up getting married because it would take too long. My mother didn't want us to get married because we were too young.

Well, guess what? In July 1954 we were married. I didn't get down on one knee to propose or anything. We just decided that it was time. If you're married and you're in the service, you get a little more money (not much) and you can live off base.

I came home on a short leave and we got married in Philly. Our wedding was actually delayed a little bit because Sara's cousin was in a car accident on the way to the wedding (it was OK, no one was hurt).

Our honeymoon was in Wildwood, N.J. We actually met one of the guys from the wedding party down there. It was funny to see him on our honeymoon!

Sara with her mother on our wedding day.

Sara on our wedding day.

Our entire wedding party and some family/guests.

Sincere thanks
for your
lovely gift

Andy and Sara Cacco

After the wedding!

Years before, back when we lived in New York, I'd said to my father, "Papà, when do the brains come in? How do you know things?"

Papà answered, "You'll just know...you'll find out."

I hadn't really thought that was a good answer, but that was the only answer that I got. It hit me on my wedding day...all of a sudden, I had responsibilities! I had better have some brains.

A couple of years later, when Sara was pregnant with Andy, my father said to me, "They're coming in!" I knew exactly what he was talking about. He was right...the brains came in when I had to take care of other people. That's when I had responsibilities!

In order to get back to Texas with my new wife, I bought Americo's 1950 Ford. He claimed, "I'm giving it to you for less than it's worth, that's your wedding present."

From Wildwood, we headed back to Texas. Remember, it's July, so it's hot...and hotter in Texas.

We started across the country and stopped in Chicago (actually, Rochelle, Ill.) to see my mother's sister (my aunt) and her sister. We had seen them once in New York, so we figured we would repay the visit and stopped on our way to Texas.

We left Chicago and headed south for Texas.

Back then, cars didn't have air conditioning. You rolled down the windows, and that was it. When we got down into Texas, Sara was not happy with the heat. "Stop the car," she shouted.

There was nothing but corn fields for as far as the eye could see, but I stopped.

I asked, "Do you really want to stop here, or should I keep driving?"

We found a gas station, got a Coke, and kept on driving.

My mother's (Barbara), sister's family in Chicago (in other words, my aunt's family in Chicago).

We got a room off the base with Mrs. Flannigan. We had a shared bath in the hall. That arrangement only lasted about a month, because I used to wake up in the morning and find the mail on the nightstand next to the bed. Mrs. Flannigan used to come into our room during the night! I wasn't going to have any of that!!

We rented another place for $80 a month – a first floor. A buddy of mine from the service, Charlie Pucket, rented the second floor.

Shortly after we got married, Sara got a job working in the Courthouse for a little while, but that didn't make me too happy, because I felt it was my job to provide for my wife.

My sergeant liked me. He used to call me "Little Shit". Before I was married, I used to sign my paycheck over to him each payday. During the month, he and I would go all over together and he would always pay. Whatever I made didn't come close to covering what he actually paid to have me hanging around. Of course, that stopped once I was married.

I'd become a pretty good airplane mechanic in six to eight months. I'd learned as much as I could. I minded my own business. My plan was to just be quiet for four years and stay out of trouble.

Towards the end of 1954, my sergeant, Sergeant Abbott, who was a crew chief, said, "Airman, how would you like to be my assistant? Put your tools away and come with me." This was the biggest compliment that I could receive.

The jobs of crew chief and assistant crew chief are like one job. Between the two of you, you are 100% responsible for one of those B-36 planes. We had a scooter that we used to move around the base, go out on the flight line, pick up a part, whatever we needed.

When the plane was in the air, we'd be off-duty. When the plane was on the ground, we were working.

When the plane landed, we'd meet the plane, get a report from the pilot, and find out if there was anything that needed to be done to the plane. We had to fix any issues *immediately* because that plane had to be ready to fly again as quickly as possible.

One day, there was a sandstorm headed our direction. This was a bad thing, and the planes had to get in the air to escape the storm. Unfortunately, two of the engines weren't working on our plane.

"Sergeant, that plane can't go, two of the engines aren't working."

"It's OK...they still have eight."

In my head I thought, "Then why do they usually have to have 10?!"

"My" plane – we always worked on the same one.

We cleared that plane out of there before the sandstorm hit.

In reality, the plane only needed all 10 engines to take-off when it was fully loaded. Once it was in the air, they'd even shut down some of the engines. That meant that an empty plane evading a sandstorm could take off easily without two of its engines.

There were times when I would be the "CQ" for the night. "Charge of Quarters". This was the person who stays awake all night – just to make sure that everything is OK.

One of these nights, when things were quiet, I was sitting around calculating how much I was paying in rent a year. It was a lot. When I multiplied it out by how long I still had left to serve, it became a whole lot of money. I began wondering why I was paying someone else, and I wasn't getting anything out of it except for a place to sleep. I wasn't building up any equity or anything.

I started looking for a trailer that we could buy, and you know when you look, you find.

Soon after that, probably the end of 1954 or the beginning of 1955, I passed by a place where they were building new homes. They were down to the last house. Sitting there was a trailer with a "For Sale" sign on it that the builder used themselves as an office while they were building the houses. It was a 36 foot Anderson trailer.

One day, I stopped in and asked what they wanted for the trailer. $1,800 was the answer. I asked the guy if I could put $500 down, then pay it off over time, $50 per month. I also asked him if I paid it completely off within a year, would he waive the interest. He thought about it and said, "Sure."

The trailer was mine, and I moved it to Grey's Trailer Park, 420 Roberts Cutoff there in Fort Worth where I rented a trailer pad and hookup. Sara and I had our first home!

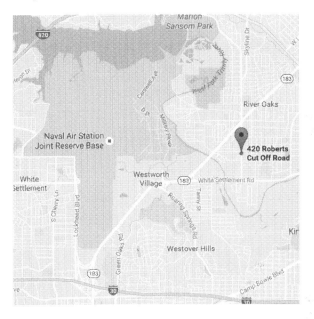

420 Roberts Cutoff was just east of Carswell AFB.

My 1950 Ford and the 36' Anderson trailer.

The guy was still working on that house, finishing it off. Every month, I'd go by the house with my payment. I got comfortable just walking into the house, dropping the money off, and heading back out. One day, I stopped by to make my payment and I walked right in, as I always did. I walked right into the living room, and I can see a woman in the kitchen cooking. OOPS! The house had been sold! I backed out of the house as fast as I could. I didn't want to get shot for trespassing. When I got back outside, I rang the doorbell. When the woman answered, she said that yes, this was her house now, and that the builder could be found at some other address. I went off and found the new place to drop off my payment!

Cocco Andrew (Sara) USAF h8430½ Delmar

Listing from the Fort Worth phone directory in 1955

I didn't want to pay the guy any interest, so I called my dad and asked him to send me $900, so that I could pay the trailer off within the year interest-free. He sent it to me, then I paid my dad off over a bit more time, but I never had to pay the guy who sold me the trailer any interest.

I wanted to learn more English, so I enrolled in night school at Texas Christian University. My professor was Betsy Bell. The first night of class, she says that everyone needs a little dictionary. I figured the bigger the dictionary, the better, so I bought the library dictionary that was about six inches thick! I still have it today.

After about two weeks of class, Professor Bell asked us to write a 1,000-word essay. I didn't know 500 words TOTAL, much less being able to write a 1,000-word essay! Well, I wrote it – or tried to. At least, I turned something in.

The next week, she said, "Mr. Cocco, I'd like to speak with you after class."

After everyone had gone, I went up to her. She began with, "I've been a professor for 30 years and I have never seen anyone massacre the English language as much as you did in this paper."

I explained to her that I'd only been in the country five or six years, and that I was in the class to try to improve my English. She felt so bad that she began giving me extra help after class.

The entire 7th Wing under General LeMay (two squadrons) went to Morocco for about four months in 1955 to resurface runways there. That was the end of my private tutoring with Betsy Bell. Sara was pregnant with Andy. She stayed with another couple while I was away.

While we were in Morocco, my Colonel (the commanding officer of my squadron) came up to me and asked, "You come from Italy, don't you?"

"Yes, sir. I came to America in 1948."

"While we're in Morocco, would you like to visit your family in Italy?"

Sara and me (and Andy) in Fort Worth, Texas.

"I sure would, sir!"

"Great. While we're there, I'll arrange for you to go."

"Can I take a buddy with me?"

"Sure."

When we were in Morocco, sure enough, my orders came through for some time off, and transport to Italy. My buddy, Johnny, and I reported to the flight that was going to take us first to Marseille, France (then we would catch a train to Italy).

We arrived at the appointed hour, all set for our trip, only to be "bumped" off the plane by a 1-Star General. When my Colonel saw me back, he asked what the heck I was doing there. I explained. Well, the Colonel called back over and said to the guy, "I'm sending Cocco back over tomorrow, and NO ONE bumps him from that flight!"

Needless to say, we made the flight to Marseille the next morning.

During our layover in France, we went to a bar to kill some time. We'd been told not to speak to any civilians, so I was trying to mind my own business when the guy next to me (who wasn't in uniform) tries to strike up a conversation. I was trying to not answer when he pulled an ID out of his pocket and showed it to me.

"You can talk to me, I'm a Captain of a Neptune. You Italian?" (the Neptune was a plane that searched for subs, and he was the pilot of that plane).

"Yes, yes, I am."

"Do you speak Italian?" he asked.

"Yes," I replied.

"How about I fly you to Venice? I need to get my hours to keep my certification. You can spend the day with me and be my translator."

So, we found ourselves on a private plane on our way to Venice. We spent the day there, then took a train to Rome.

I stopped in at my godmother's house to pay them a visit. By this time, Leandro had a phone back in Ferentino, so I decided to give him a call.

"How are you doing?" I asked when he picked up the phone.

"Who is this?"

"Don't you recognize your own brother's voice?" I quipped, and we made plans for us to come out to Ferentino on the train for a visit.

My godmother wanted to make sure that I took something nice back to the states for my wife, so she took me shopping – at a jewelry store. I didn't want to tell her that I really had no money, so she picked out a lovely 18K gold bracelet that cost about $300 – all the money I had.

We took the train from Rome to Ferentino, and the whole family met us at the station!

Me (center) with two of my buddies from Ferentino.

Indoor plumbing had come to our house, but the toilet paper was 'old school'. That meant that the toilet paper consisted of strips of cut-up paper hanging from a nail in the bathroom!

By this time, Leandro had a son. We took a day and went to the beach.

My cousins, Joe and Mary, at their house.

Uncle Augusto and his wife (Note: During the first bombing of our area during WWII, I hid under the stairs there to the right of my uncle).

Me (on left), Leandro, and my nephew, Peter, at the beach.

We stayed in Ferentino four or five days and had a terrific visit.

During the years since we'd left, Leandro had become an

insurance agent and ran his own agency. He had three sons:

Pietro (Peter) was born shortly after we left Italy. He grew up to become a successful doctor, a gynecologist.

Massimo, his second son, became a prominent Ferentino attorney.

Flavio ended up taking over his father's insurance agency.

Emanuela, Massimo's daughter, also became an attorney like her father.

My grandchildren (Michelle and Drew) and Leandro at a natural spring water fountain in Supino.

Johnny and I were flying back to Morocco out of Naples, so we hopped on the train and headed south. My buddy had family in Avellino, Italy, which was on the way to Naples. We decided to stop off and visit with his family on our way.

When we got to Avellino, we grabbed a cab and told the cabbie where we wanted to go, and who we were going to see. The cabbie realized that we really didn't want to go INTO Avellino, but that the people we wanted to visit were outside of the city. He drove us right to the house – way out in the country.

When I saw the house, I recognized the area for what it was. It was just like our home in Ferentino used to be. No electricity, no indoor plumbing. We were supposed to stay three or four days, but as I got out of the car, I told the cabbie to pick us up that night.

When Johnny had to use "the facilities", he asked where they were. I laughed and pointed, and said 'pick a bush'. He almost fainted! When the cab showed up that night to pick us up, he was overjoyed. He had never experienced that kind of primitive living, and was happy to leave.

Off we went to Naples where we caught a plane back to Casablanca.

Christmas 1955 arrived and Sara and I had no money. I told Sara not to buy me anything because I wasn't not buying her anything. We just didn't have anything extra. She gave me a watch with a diamond at 12, 3, 6 and 9. She got a sweater. She was mad, but I'd warned her! We didn't even have the money to buy a chicken for dinner. Chicken was $1.57 (not a pound, but for the entire chicken). We could come up with $1.45. Sara rooted around in her handbag and came up with another 12¢. We had chicken for Christmas dinner. (Sidenote: My son, Mike, has that watch now).

That same Christmas, my buddy, Charlie Pucket, went out and bought six or eight items for his wife for Christmas. He had to pay $2.00 every payday until he paid it off, but he had gifts at Christmas for his wife. I didn't go for that baloney! I didn't spend money I didn't have.

Because we never had any money, I always had a part-time job, in addition to being in the Air Force.

One day, I saw a guy selling religious articles. I asked him what he was doing. He told me and asked if I wanted to help him. Sure! I went to the Spanish section of Fort Worth and sold out of the articles in a month and a half! The guy was amazed.

The hanger that we worked out of was large, but not large enough to hold the plane itself. It did, however, hold everything else. Everything and anything that we needed. One day, I saw a guy taking money out of the cigarette machine and filling the machine back up with cigarettes.

I walked over to him and said, "Mr. Clear, don't you think you're too old to be doing that?"

"You want to do it?"

"I'd be happy to."

He gave me his card, and told me to come over to his house on Sunday. He'd cook some nice steaks, and we'd discuss things. When I got to his house on Sunday, he was busy already working with the steaks.

"Would you do me a favor?" he asked.

"Sure."

"Would you count those quarters that are on the counter?"

So, I sat down and counted. At the end, he asked me how much was there, and I told him.

We sat down and had a nice dinner.

On Monday, he came by the base and asked me what my schedule was like.

"How'd you like to fill the cigarette and ice cream machines from Fort Worth to Dallas?"

One of the stops on my route was the Colonial Country Club in

Fort Worth. I had never seen anything as ritzy in my life. "So," I thought, "this is how the other half lives." I never imagined that years from then, I would actually play on some of those swanky golf courses!

I'd be gone for 10-14 hours when I was out on my route. I kept that job until I was discharged from the service.

My boss asked me where I was going when I told him I was leaving.

"I'm going back to Philly. It's time I start my life."

He said, "I'll give you six months. If you want to come back, I'll make you my partner!"

Sara had Andy in Texas on February 1, 1956.

Andy in Texas.

When my sergeant retired in 1956, I became the crew chief. Promotions were frozen, so I didn't really have enough stripes to be a crew chief, but I was one.

My job was a very serious one. You couldn't make any mistakes. You were handling bombs.

The B-36 hydrogen bomb.

The B-36 planes could carry two hydrogen bombs, or 150 500-pound bombs in their bay. When they were carrying the 500 pound bombs, the plane could carpet-bomb an area of a few miles. The airman would hit a button to initiate the launch sequence, and the plane would do the rest, releasing the bombs in a sequence as they flew.

Sara was pregnant again and due to have Michael in 1957. I knew that I was getting out soon, so I took a leave in February of 1957 and moved Sara, Andy and the not-yet-born Michael back to Philly. Sara and Andy (and, of course, Michael) stayed with her parents because there was no room at my parents' house. I went back to Carswell to finish the last few months of service.

**Back at Carswell many years later with one of the
bombs we loaded.**

Michael was born in March 1957 at the Philadelphia Naval
Hospital (he cost me $17 to be born) while I was down in Texas.

I was ready to be discharged in July 1957. The B-36 planes were
being replaced by the B-52's. My colonel offered me a B-52 and a
$10,000 bonus and a stripe (a promotion in rank) to stay in the
service (which was a boatload of money in 1957).

I said to the colonel, "Did I do a good job?"

"You did an excellent job. That's why we'll pay you $10,000 to
stay! It'll cost $100,000 to train someone to replace you. We'd
rather keep you here!"

"Well, I'm ready to go home now. I like the Air Force, but I don't
like the hurry up and wait. It's time for me to go."

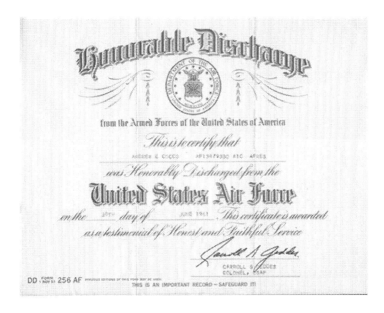

USAF Discharge Certificate – June 30, 1961.

Before I headed home to my family, I had to sell the trailer we were living in. Remember, I'd bought it for $1,800. I was able to sell it for $1,500! I thought that ending up paying $300 for our housing for over two years was a pretty good deal.

I went to U-Haul to find out how much it would cost to rent a trailer to get our possessions from Fort Worth to Philadelphia. I was shocked when they told me $200 or $300. You must be kidding! "You're a mechanic, Cocco, just think!" I told myself.

I bought an axle and two wheels at a junkyard for a couple of bucks. I welded angle irons to the axle and put on lights. I made a bed of plywood and added brakes. When I was done, the trailer cost me about $25-$30. I loaded up all our belongings and headed home. Once back in Philly, I sold the little, hand-made trailer for $150! And U-Haul was going to charge me a couple of hundred!

BACK HOME IN PHILLY

As I was finishing up my time at Carswell, I started to think about what I wanted to do after I was discharged. I was a pretty good airplane mechanic, and enjoyed that work, so I decided to go to school, one night a week, to get my civilian license to work on the airframe of the commercial planes.

I got home and started looking for a job right away. I went down to Island Avenue where TWA had a big facility and applied for a job. They hired me right away at the sum of $5.75/hour (which was a lot of money), but I was going to have to move to L.A. or somewhere else. Not gonna happen. Time to keep looking.

A friend of my in-laws, Frank DeFeo, owned DeFeo Wireworks. DeFeo Wireworks, founded in 1957, made pretty much anything out of wire.

A lot of what they did was display dispensers. For instance, they made the wire displays that dispensed Krylon paint cans. Frank DeFeo hired me to do piecework. The more pieces I put together, the more money I made.

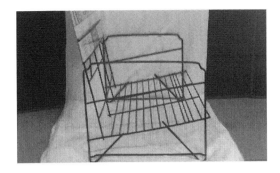

Side view of a Krylon display like those we assembled at the Wireworks.

This is a nail polish rack like those we assembled at Wireworks.

Once I learned the job, I liked it. Every day was a little different because the jigs you were putting together were different. Some days, it was Krylon displays. Other days, it was the backpieces for a Mummer's String Band!

Frank's son, Peter worked for his father in the business, but didn't like it. He was an artist and wanted to design, but the shop needed someone to really organize it and streamline the production. The first week, Peter quit to go pursue his dreams.

One day, I figured out that the assembly of one item was more complicated than it had to be. I modified the jig, and found that we could make twice as many in the same period of time. When you're being paid by the piece, that improvement is huge!

Another day, I approached Frank and told him that I could run the shop AND assemble the items. He would then be able to go out and get more work for the shop. He decided to pay me $40/week for being a supervisor, then I'd still get the 10¢ per piece for each of the baskets that I assembled.

When a captain from the Ferko String Band showed up one day with a cardboard sample of his design for the big Mummer's backpieces, he and I sat down to figure out how to make them. It was a pair of butterfly wings. I figured out how to convert that cardboard cutout into a wire frame that would work for them on January 1st as they marched down Broad Street. I loved this type of work because it was project-based work and not timed work. I got to use my creativity and ingenuity to solve the customer's problem. In the end, we had 60 pretty neat pairs of butterfly wings that the band could wear fastened to their backs, and that wouldn't interfere with them playing their music. Peter DeFeo, Franks' son, sent me congratulations on the work.

The shop was in Hunting Park, up in North Philly. We were living in West Philly. My family needed to get out of my in-laws' house. Frank told me that he was going to be moving the shop to Lansdowne, so we began looking for a house in that area.

Sara made it clear that she didn't want to raise the kids in a driveway in the city. She wanted a yard where they could play.

In 1958, we found our house at 2338 Mole Lane in Secane, Pa. It's the house we still live in today. We put down $1,000 (left over from the sale of the trailer), and promptly rented the house out because we couldn't afford to furnish it yet.

Finally, in February or March of 1959, we moved into our very own house.

No sooner had we moved into the new house, then Frank said to me, "I've got you now. You have a wife, two kids and a mortgage. You can't leave. I'm taking the $40 per week away, you're going to have to earn it back through the piecework."

2338 Mole Lane in 1959.

...and today...we're still in the same house.

Well, I can tell you that I was EXTREMELY upset. Here I'd given him my all, I'd improved the efficiency of his shop, allowed him to increase his sales, and my "thank you" was a pay cut. I was panicked. I was *barely* making it WITH the $40. Without it, I couldn't pay the bills.

Heading home, I was despondent. I stopped on Lancaster
Avenue at Sealtest Dairies to pick up a milk route. You'd get up
in the middle of the night and deliver the milk to the homes, then
you'd go by each house at the end of the week, collect the money
they owed you, and try to 'upsell' the homeowners with other
'goodies'. It wasn't a very good prospect, but it was something.

I had gotten friendly with my neighbor in Secane, George
Gothier. George was an Electrolux salesman. When he asked me
what was the matter, I told him what had happened. He couldn't
believe it.

I told him that I was going to pick up the job with Sealtest and he
said, "You're not going to do that. You're going to become a
salesman. I want you to go into the insurance business." I
thought that that was the craziest thing I'd heard. I wasn't a
salesman and I knew nothing about insurance...but George
wasn't taking 'no' for an answer.

Meeting George Gothier was another big fork in my Road of Life.

JOHN HANCOCK

George decided that he was going to show me that I COULD be a
salesman. On Saturday, he took me out to Valley Forge where a
bunch of new split-level homes were being built. He told me to
go knock on doors, and sell a vacuum. Well, I sold one before he
did that morning! George finally convinced me to apply at the
insurance companies in the area.

He gave me the addresses of Prudential, John Hancock and
Metropolitan. First, I went to Prudential at 54th and City Line
Avenue to apply for a job. Next, I headed to John Hancock in
Lansdowne, where George had told me to ask for a Mr. Charlie
Schenk.

I have to step back again, and sort of set up the situation. It was
July 1959 and it was HOT!! I only had a nice winter jacket and a

string tie. I didn't want to look like a bum in my other clothes, so I suffered through wearing a heavy, wool coat in the middle of summer. I must have looked a sight!

When I walked into the office, I asked to speak to Mr. Schenk. When he came out, I told him that I was looking for a job selling insurance. He asked, "Who sent you?"

"My neighbor, George Gothier."

Laughing, Mr. Schenk replied, "Is that guy out of jail already?"

He continued on to say that he didn't have any openings, but that I should go to the Fidelity Building in Chester at 5th and Market streets and I should ask to see Mr. Buckley. "Tell him that I sent you, and don't take no for an answer. I know he has openings."

It was very late in the day, and I was hot and depressed, but off I went from Lansdowne to 5th and Market in Chester, and I asked to speak with Mr. Buckley.

When I was in front of him, I bravely declared, "Mr. Charlie Schenk sent me, and told me not to leave until you gave me a job."

"Did he really?" replied Mr. Buckley. "What's your accent? Italian?" Of course, I answered "Yes."

"Italians are hardworking people."

I was honest. I told him that I didn't know anything about insurance.

"OK," he says. "Do you know where 35 East Plumstead Avenue is in Lansdowne? Be there at 5 p.m."

I showed up at his home at 35 East Plumstead Avenue in Lansdowne at 5 p.m. Mr. Buckley was there with a bunch of forms. We went into his dining room. He told me to fill in my name and address. He showed me a few boxes to check and mark, and on the last page was a math problem. I'm good at math, but reading the problem was another matter. I guess I took too long to fill it in because he gave me the answers, then had me sign at the bottom of the form. When that was all done, he said, "You've got a job. Come into the office on Monday morning. You have to study for the exam."

Years later, when I held the same position as Mr. Buckley and Mr. Schenk did when I first started, I figured out that they actually disliked one another – a lot. Mr. Schenk had sent me to Mr. Buckley as a joke. Schenk had four or five openings in his office when I'd applied, but he wasn't about to hire me, the "Guinea". You would NEVER send someone you thought might be good to your competitor.

Mr. Schenk had three sons who all worked in the insurance business, but they couldn't work in their father's office, so they worked in other offices in the area.

Mr. Buckley called his bluff. Buckley figured he'd prove Schenk wrong. Boy, did he! Mr. Schenk tried to make me the brunt of a joke, but Mr. Buckley really liked me. Later on, Schenk tried to take credit for "finding me", but Mr. Buckley would have none of that. Over the years, Mr. Buckley treated me almost like part of the family.

It was our job to sell the insurance, but it was also our job to collect the money (weekly or monthly). That took a lot of time. I made money selling, not collecting, so some of my customers would get in arrears. Mr. Buckley would holler at me saying, "You're nothing but a bum!" because I wouldn't be up-to-date with my collections. Mrs. Buckley said, "He hollers at you, but you're his 24-karat bum!" I was a pall-bearer at both his funeral and that of his wife.

Mr. Buckley already knew a lesson that I was to learn. If you think someone is good, you find a job for them…you don't let them go…you don't let them walk out! Through the years, I tried to follow that same gut instinct.

As soon as I was hired, I made a beeline for George and told him that I got the job. George said, "Did you ask what area you'd be covering?" Of course, I hadn't thought to ask. I ended up getting the area near Secane, around Fairview Road and Route 420.

I studied for the insurance exam for the next two weeks, while I continued to work at Wireworks. I didn't have a lot of formal schooling, but I studied hard, and I passed the Life and Health Insurance test, so I was good to start my new career.

My license to sell insurance in Pennsylvania.

Once I passed the exam, I went in to Frank DeFeo to give my two-week's notice. Somehow, I knew he wouldn't let me work out the time. I walked in and said, "I'm quitting." He replied, "You'll never make it selling insurance. Get out of here." That was the end of that. I was now working for John Hancock.

When Mary DeFeo, Frank's wife, found out that I was leaving Wireworks, she told him that letting me leave was the worst mistake he'd made in his life. He needed me.

I was terrified. I was leaving about $140/week (about $100 from the piecework, plus the $40 for supervising in the shop), and I was going to $57/week plus commissions. I could barely live on the $140/week, much less on only $57/week, and it was going to take a while until I actually saw ANY commissions in the form of a check.

When I started, I was assigned to a staff manager. Each staff manager had 10 salesmen under him. The staff manager that I was assigned to, Charlie Hughes, took me around, introduced me to the territory and helped me get started selling. He'd actually do some of the selling for me because I was so green, I didn't know anything. The staff manager's job is to get you up-to-speed quickly so that you start making money sooner, rather than later.

Once I sold something, I had to write-up an application and submit it to the underwriter. If the application was approved, then it was submitted to billing, and after that it was paid. Only when the bill was paid by the customer did I get a commission. That whole process could take a couple of months. I was hurting for money.

There were very few telephones, so the only way to make the sale was to knock on doors. I knocked and knocked on doors. I got rejection after rejection. I knew I had to make a living, so I just kept at it. It was the hardest thing that I ever did. I HATED the rejections, but I kept going.

One woman in Folsom blasted me, in Italian, because I had interrupted her cooking dinner. I left with my tail between my legs. I had walked down the street a little way, then stopped because I realized that if I let that get to me, I'd be out of the insurance business soon. I turned around and went back to her door and said, in Italian, that I was terribly sorry for the intrusion, but that I had a family to support, and that I was just working to pay my bills. She let me in. You just had to keep knocking on those doors to get to one that might allow you to make the sale.

With a lot of work knocking on door after door after door, I started to eek out a living. There was nothing extra, and nothing could go wrong, or I couldn't pay for it, but I was paying the basic bills and the mortgage. When my daughter, Linda, was born in March 1961, I couldn't afford to pay the doctor. The bill came from the doctor's office, but I had to ignore it. Finally, when Linda was about two years old, I had some money, so I dug out the bill, tacked on some interest and sent the payment – in full – to the doctor.

**I got Gypsy about the time I started at John Hancock.
She was a faithful companion for 16 years.**

Meanwhile, while I was trying to get going selling insurance, my
brother, Americo, had started a nursery on Route 420. I
volunteered my time and helped him for five or six months (as
long as the nursery lasted) whenever I had free time, to help him
make a go of his place.

When the nursery didn't pan out, he gave it up and got a job as a
machinist at a shop on routes 3 and 926. Americo still wanted to
own his own business, so he and another guy, Frank G. Wilson,

who was an inventor, rented a barn out in Paoli. My brother had the tools to handle some small jobs, but he still worked as a machinist at the other shop. If there was extra work, I'd help out in my free time.

Linda's baptism, April 15, 1961. Me, my mother and father.

Americo's shop grew and he and Frank moved from the barn to King Street in Paoli. Americo quit the other job. He was starting to get somewhere! I figured that once he became successful, he would hire me to come along.

Unfortunately, Americo didn't see it that way. He used to tell me, "You're neither cooked nor raw." He put me down because I didn't have a good education. The bad thing was that I started to believe him when he said that I wasn't going to amount to anything. I really wanted his approval.

I managed to sell my brother a $10,000 policy, but I had to buy him a carton of VO whiskey to get him to do it. Why was he so tough on me?

Americo's shop made parts for Westinghouse (among other things). I would deliver the parts and bring my brother the receipt. As his shop grew, he was able to buy a pickup truck. I thought I could do the deliveries in that truck, but Americo told me that Carl (one of the other guys in his shop) could do it. I didn't get that work.

I'm still thinking that Americo is going to take me with him as he grew more successful, yet when the opportunities came to include me, he didn't.

I always tried to help him out where I could. I kept hoping that he would see the value in me.

One day, I stopped into see him, and his best friend, Joe, stopped in, as well. It was warm, and I said to Joe, "Why don't you take off your jacket?"

Joe replied, "I'm only allowed 20 minutes here." Joe knew the boundaries with Americo better than I did.

GOLF

Mr. Buckley, my boss, put out a challenge to the salesmen in the office in the summer of 1960. He said that he'd take whomever the top-selling agents for the next three weeks were to play a round of golf at Rolling Green Golf Club.

Guess who was one of the winners? Yup...me. I didn't have clubs. I didn't have shoes. I didn't know anything at all about golf, but I was going to play. I asked everyone I knew if they had any clubs or shoes, and finally, Sara's cousin said that he had a few clubs in the garage, but no shoes. He let me borrow the clubs.

Rolling Green Golf Course

Back in 1960, Italians weren't even allowed to walk into Rolling Green, but I was going to play with my boss. Rolling Green was an "exclusive" club.

Well, the day came to play and I pulled into the lot and parked. Mr. Buckley was on the porch and watched me get out of my car, then watched me pull the ratty bag of clubs from the trunk. He started yelling, "STOP" from the porch, and bolted across the parking lot to my car screaming, "Get the hell back in that car. Wait here. Don't move until I get back!" He was my boss, so I obeyed and got back in the car.

After a little while, I saw him coming back across the parking lot with a bag full of clubs and some shoes. Mr. Buckley came up to me and said, "Wait here. A kid will come out and say 'Can I help you, sir?', and you will say, 'Thank you', then give him the clubs and shoes. Follow him and we'll go play some golf."

Sure enough, the kid came over, I handed him my clubs and shoes, and my first round of golf began!

Pretty decent shot of me on a golf course many years later.

IT'S A HELL OF A LIFE!

JOHN HANCOCK HONOR CLUB

In 1960, John Hancock started the 'Honor Club'. The Honor Club was to recognize the top-selling agents in the company. I made the Honor Club that very first year!

The Honor Club was held at the very exclusive Greenbrier Resort in West Virginia.

The Greenbrier Resort

To get to the resort, the Greenbrier added a private train car. We rode that across the state to Greenbrier, W.V., and arrived in style.

The Greenbrier Resort is fancy. I'd never seen anything like it. President Truman used to vacation there. It was gorgeous. I had to tip four guys just to get from the front door to my room! Amazingly, I had a room all to myself. Every room was different. All of the staff dressed differently, in period costumes. It was all I could do not to stare at everything.

Greenbrier Colonnade Dining Room.

Our first dinner was in the Colonnade Dining Room.

We had chicken for dinner, and I was going to get every last little bit from the bones. I was a fast eater (still am). As I was finishing up, a guy approached me with a towel on his arm and a dish filled with water. I waved him off as if I were still eating. A few minutes later, I see him approach someone else. When I see them dip their hands in the water, then dry them on the towel, I knew what to do! The next time the guy was in my area, I let him come over and acted like I knew exactly what to do with a finger bowl!

I was TOTALLY out of my league!

THE 1960'S CONTINUE

Things were going OK. Not great, but OK. I really hated the rejections I had to get. They started to wear on me. By this time, I was probably making $10,000 or $12,000 a year.

Speaking at an Honor Club event.

My car was essential to my success because I had to drive all around. In 1962 or 1963, I had an old car (a 1956 Dodge). I was down in Chester one day and I broke down right in front of Murphy Ford. A guy came out to see if he could help me, but it was obvious that there was nothing he could do. My car had died. He asked me, "Who's your boss?" I told him, Mr. Buckley. He went off for a little while, then came back and told me, "Your boss says he'll take responsibility." I was able to drive off the lot with a brand new car! Mr. Buckley was smart. He knew I'd work even harder to pay off the car and not let him down.

I'd become the 'Office Debit Agent' which is the agent for those folks who didn't want or have their own agent. They may have called in and bought the policy, or they wanted to come in to the office and pay, rather than having someone show up at their door. I should explain that a 'debit' is an agent's book of business. So, the 'Office Debit' was the book of business not assigned to a specific agent. I was that guy.

When I took the Office Debit job, I brought one of my buddies,

Dick Miranda in to sell insurance. Dick was working at Korvette's (a department store in Springfield), and I knew he could earn more selling insurance than he was making at the store.

Dick started at John Hancock, and I showed him the ropes. We would go out on calls together. When that happens, you're supposed to work the customer together, and share in the commission. Dick would go back to the house without me, then come back and tell me that HE had written this new business...not giving me any credit for the help that I'd given him.

Dick, his wife, Sara and I would go out to dinner or bowl together. Dick's wife started prying and asking Sara, "How much did Andy sell last year?" Bringing him into John Hancock sort of broke up the friendship.

By now, I had really learned to play golf. I realized how important it was to being successful in business. I kept bugging Americo, telling him that he needed to learn how to play. He replied that golf was nothing but hitting a stupid, white ball. Finally, he agreed to go to a driving range with me out on Route 3 to see what golf was all about.

Out at the range, Americo put his ball down and swung. Whiff! He tried again. Whiff! He tried a third time and hit the ball about 10 yards. I put my ball down and drove it about 200 yards! Well, Americo didn't like that. He left the range that day, but went back to a driving range, by himself, and worked and worked to get better. One day, he called me and invited me to play a round of golf in Paoli. I went up and we played. Americo lost, but he'd gotten a lot better.

I recommended that he join a private club because it would really help his business. I had friends, my clients, who belonged to Springhaven Golf Club. They said that they would sponsor Americo if he wanted to join. For once, he actually listened to me and he joined based on the sponsorship of my clients.

Americo learned that you could really schmooze on a golf course. He got so many jobs on the course that he started making some serious money. By the time 1966/67 rolled around, he was delivering color TV's to the guys at Westinghouse (one of his best clients) as a 'thank you'. For some reason, he'd stopped in to see me when he was on his way to deliver them. I asked him if I could have one of the TV's because I still had an old one with tubes. Americo replied, "What do you think they are? Peanuts?" Needless to say, I didn't get a TV.

Still, in my mind, I thought that Americo was going to take me along with him when he got <u>really</u> big. I was going to be able to stop selling insurance and stop being rejected. He was going to call me up one day and say, "Stop selling insurance and come join me." Sara said to me, "He's never going to ask you. He doesn't like you." Well, I certainly didn't like hearing that.

Around 1968, Frank Wilson, who shared the space with Americo, had gotten a patent on a new mop head. Officially, it was a 'wringer mop head replacement and actuator mechanism'. When Frank asked me if I wanted to invest $1,000 in the mop, I said, "Yes". It was a great idea, and I knew he'd do well with it. Unfortunately, he went bust.

In July 1969, John Hancock went on strike. I was panicked. I had a bunch of bills to pay and no money coming in. By this time, I was making about $200/week. I went to Americo to ask him if I could work for him while we were out on strike. He offered me $125/week which just wasn't going to cut it. I told him what I needed to make, and he said, no, he couldn't pay any more. When I asked if I could stay late and make up the difference on piecework, Americo replied that he couldn't leave me in the shop alone. WHAT? I was his brother? Did he really think that he couldn't trust me?

Now, I was upset on two fronts – I was on strike AND my brother wouldn't help me out.

In order to make it through the strike, I went to my barber, Joe

Giordano. I told him what was going on and asked him if I could borrow some money. "How much?" he asked. "How about $500?" I replied. He went in the back, came out, and handed me the money. My barber trusted me. My own brother did not. That hurt.

The strike lasted for six weeks. At the end, I went back to work.

Frank Wilson came back to me in 1969 and said, "I know you lost $1,000 with me before, but we're starting it again. You want in?"

I didn't have the money, so I asked my brother for the $1,000. He said, "You don't want to do anything with that." He didn't lend me the money.

Of course, Frank went on to be very successful with that new mop. I would have made some good money if I'd invested that $1,000 the second time.

At one point, I asked Americo straight out if I could join his business. He answered, "I wish there was enough in this business to bring you in, but there's not." There was enough to support four families, but he wasn't going to help me.

That point was hammered home when Sara and I went out to dinner – one time, only one time – with Americo and his wife. We went to the San Marco on City Line Avenue. During the meal, Americo said, "If you weren't my brother, I wouldn't even go out to eat with you." What a snob.

After that, I would stop in occasionally to see Americo, but it was never the same. I'd gotten the message.

JOHN HANCOCK - STAFF MANAGER

After the strike ended, I decided that I would take a staff manager role. I was bored with selling, and I was still hurt by the rejections.

Each office had a manager.

Under the manager, there were two or three staff managers. Each staff manager had 10 salesmen under them.

I was ready!

I was offered the staff manager job in Mr. Buckley's office, but I was ready for a change. Roy Branton, the vice president for John Hancock in our region, told me that there was an opening in the Norristown office, and that I should go to talk with Walter Duffy up there. He was the "Mr. Buckley" up in Norristown.

I went up to Norristown to meet Mr. Duffy. I told him that I had heard he had an opening for a staff manager, and I wondered why no one there wanted the job. He said that he didn't know. I responded that I would take the job as long as he was willing to go along with the following, "You don't tell me what to do; when to do it; or how to do it. At the end of six months we'll meet to evaluate my performance. If you don't like what I'm doing, I'll leave." He hired me right then and there.

At a John Hancock meeting with Roger Staubach (quarterback for the Dallas Cowboys).

My area of responsibility went from Conshohocken to Spring City. I went into the office to report to Mr. Duffy once a week, but basically, he left me alone, despite "everyone" saying that I wouldn't be able to handle the job. Others said that that was as high as I would go because I didn't have a formal education.

The office had two, 10-man sales forces. I was assigned 10 guys from the salesmen in the office for my team. I made the rounds – one week with each guy – until I'd been around with all of them. 10 weeks. 10 guys. I saw who was hungry. I saw who didn't give a damn. I saw who needed some support, but was trying.

A lot of managers feel that they have "arrived" when they get that "staff manager" title. Not me. I wanted to know how they were working. I wanted to know how they got their appointments. I wanted to know their approach.

I reminded them that the existing policy holders were their best customers.

I taught them to make the last appointment of the day (8 p.m.) first and work backwards. It will keep you out on the road and productive.

I would call a current policy holder and ask them if they understood their policy. If they said, "no", then I'd tell them that I'd be in their neighborhood and could I stop by for a few minutes to explain it to them. If they said, "yes", then I'd say the same thing, but tell them that there was something new to show them on their policy. Either way, I got an appointment!

I would go in with the agents. I'd let them give the pitch themselves, then critique them once we'd left. Some guys pushed back. Others wanted me with them all the time. I found enough guys who wanted my help that I was out on the road two or three nights a week. I got to know my guys, and they got to know me.

I targeted one guy in my group by the name of Jim Vetaboli, and worked with him particularly hard between August and

IT'S A HELL OF A LIFE!

December. Jim didn't know how to sell, but he knew some local "big" families such as the Genuardi's (grocery store family) and Conicelli's (car dealerships). I knew that he could work those relationships and build a good book of business, as long as I could show him the ropes and teach him how to do it.

Jim made the President's Club, which is a higher honor than the Honor Club in 1969. That was a lot of work for a little over four months. Letters of congratulations poured in.

In 1970, I had six guys make Honor Club.

In 1971, I had nine guys make the Honor Club.

In 1972, Norristown was the number one district in the region and made the President's Club. When Mr. Duffy went up to accept the award, he said, "I will not receive this trophy by myself. We couldn't have done it without Andy Cocco."

Along comes 1973, and I'd made Honor Club personally by May, as well as, moving my team along. Things were rolling right along.

In November, Mr. Duffy called me into his office and told me to "sign this paper." I didn't know what I was signing, but my boss told me to sign it, so I signed it. It turns out that it was a sample of my signature, so that they could have a signature stamp made for me. You're wondering 'why', right?

The next day, I got a call from Roy Branton (remember, he'd sent me up to Norristown as sales manager). He said, "Listen, on Monday morning you are to report to 325 Chestnut Street to the 9th floor. You're taking over as district manager there."

Wait!! What?!?!

YOU-HAVE-GOT-TO-BE-KIDDING-ME!!!!

I asked him if he was coming down to introduce me around. He said, "No." I asked, "How will I know?" He said, "You'll know."

With Roy Branton and Sara.

Roy Branton "made" me. He believed in me. He gave me opportunities that most people never got. I have a lot to thank him for.

I'd never heard of such a thing! Before you could be a district manager, you had to be an agent, a staff manager (so far, I'd done both of those), a regional supervisor, and ONLY THEN would you be considered as a district manager, and NEVER in your own "neighborhood". You'd be shipped to New York or California, or some other place. Here I was, right in my district and I was skipping all those steps...I was going from staff manager to district manager. I was one of only 210 people in the whole country at that level in John Hancock.

The Philly office was a large one and had 30 agents, three staff managers, seven office "girls", and one Office Debit agent (which meant that it really had 31 agents). It had had three different managers in four years.

325 Chestnut Street, Philadelphia.

The sales force was all part of the AFL-CIO. I had belonged to the union until I became a staff manager. Once you become a staff manager, you're 'management' and not part of the union.

So, on Monday morning, I reported to work on the 9th floor at 325 Chestnut Street. I was nervous as hell as I headed up the elevator, but when I got off on the 9th floor I saw the doors to the offices. On those glass doors to the office was the lettering:

ANDREW E. COCCO, DISTRICT MANAGER

My official John Hancock headshot.

Andrew E. Cocco
District Manager

John Hancock Mutual Life
Insurance Company

Suite 1200
Constitution Place
325 Chestnut Street
Philadelphia, PA 19106
(215) 925-8807

Registered Representative
John Hancock Casualty, Mutual Funds
Variable Life and Annuities

District Manager business card.

[See next page for the letter from John Hancock announcing my promotion]

In I went, and walked over to the reception desk. Joan Colton, a wonderful woman, approached me and said, "May I help you, sir?"

I chuckled, pointed to the door, and said "Yes, I'm it." Joan laughed and set about giving me a tour of the office and getting me settled.

Overnight, I'd gone from making a nice salary of $22,000-$23,000 a year to making $70,000!!! I also quit smoking – even though I could now afford the cigarettes.

My philosophy, in business and in life, was that you had to show the people under you how to improve. If you don't show them how to improve, you can't help and you'll fail. I wasn't going to fail.

I used the same process as a district manager that I used as a staff manager. I figured out which were the 20% of the group who would bring in 80% of the business.

I am pretty good at reading people. I was a friend to all, not a "buddy", but everyone knew that they could come talk to me. If someone was a loner, I'd leave them alone, but if they wanted me to help them, I was more than happy to do that.

Four guys from the union came in to the office one day (the union committee reps were actually John Hancock sales reps) led by Vince Novello. He had a book in his hand that had 3-carbon copy forms in it.

After I'd introduced myself, told them a little bit about me and that I'd come from the Norristown office,I asked him, "What's in that book?"

"It's a grievance book," replied Vince.

IT'S A HELL OF A LIFE!

John Hancock Mutual Life Insurance Company

District Agency Department

Andrew A. Adinolfi, C.L.U.
Senior Vice President

200 Berkeley Street
Boston, Massachusetts 02117

October 19, 1973

CIRCULAR LETTER TO DISTRICT MANAGERS

Gentlemen:

Effective - December 1, 1973

Harry W. Silver, CLU, District Manager at the Erie, Pennsylvania District will retire under the Company's Pension Plan.

Harry began his employment as an Agent in March 1932 at the Erie District, where he was appointed Staff Manager in July 1933. After serving three years of military duty, he returned in the same capacity, and in March 1954 was appointed District Manager at the Pittsburgh East District. He assumed his present management responsibilities in August 1962.

Harry has served the Company with ever increasing dedication over the years, and we all join in wishing him the very best in the retirement years ahead.

Nicholas F. Capella, District Manager at the Media, Pennsylvania District will retire under the Company's Pension Plan.

Nick joined the Company as an Agent at the former Chicago #1 District in November 1939 where he was appointed Staff Manager in May 1940. He was appointed Regional Supervisor in the North Central Region in December 1955 and was named Manager at the Frankford West District in April 1957. He served in the same capacity at the Norristown and Mayfair Districts before transferring to the Media District in July 1967.

Throughout his career, Nick has served the Company with the highest degree of dedication, and we are all grateful for his many fine contributions.

Andrew E. Cocco, Staff Manager at the Norristown District has been appointed District Manager at the Independence Square, Pennsylvania District.

Andy began his career with the John Hancock in August 1959
as an Agent in the former Chester, Pennsylvania District.
He was appointed Staff Manager at the Norristown District
in July 1970.

Andy has qualified five times for the President's Club and
thirteen times for the Regional Honor Club.

All of us extend to Andy our sincere wishes for continued
success in his future endeavors.

Anthony J. Sparacino, Regional Supervisor in the East Central
Region, has been appointed District Manager at the Erie,
Pennsylvania District.

Tony began his association with the John Hancock in June 1960
as an Agent at the Pittsburgh East District, where he was
appointed Staff Manager in February 1963. He transferred to
the McKeesport, Pennsylvania District in April 1969 before
joining the Mid-Atlantic Regional Organization in March 1970.
He assumed his present duties in January 1973.

Tony is a one time qualifier for the President's Club and
nine time qualifier for the Regional Honor Club.

We wish Tony every success as he undertakes his new responsibilities.

Russell F. Miller, CLU, District Manager at the Independence
Square District, will transfer to the Media, Pennsylvania
District.

Effective Immediately ---

Gene B. Stowe, District Manager at the Greensboro, North
Carolina District, has resigned and will remain with the
Company in another capacity.

Sincerely,

Andrew A. Adenoff.

Senior Vice President

(EXTRA COPIES FOR THE STAFF MANAGERS)

Presented with appreciation to

ANDREW E. COCCO
for his continued
distinguished sales achievements

August 1975

One of the awards that I won – this one in 1975.

"What's that?" I asked.

He proceeded to tell me that when there was an issue, it went into the book in triplicate: one copy for the union, one for me and one for an arbitrator.

"Listen," I said, "If we have any problems and we need outsiders to tell us who's right, then I'm the first guy who should be fired, and you, Vince, are the second guy who should be fired!"

I continued by saying, "We have 7,000 square feet of office space here. We have 45 people working here. If we don't make the numbers, none of us will be here. It's that easy."

"If you want to leave me a part of that book, then maybe I can write something down in it, too! Look, I will work with you and help you. We shouldn't have any issues."

For the 16 years that I ran that office, we never had a grievance. Not one.

My two favorite "girls" – Joan Colton and Marie Nighita.

I began working with the people under me, and things started improving. The union committee reps started making the Honor Club. The office was getting better and better. People farther up the chain noticed. Philly was on the map!

After I'd watched the office staff work, I picked the assistant office supervisor, Joan Colton (the same woman who had greeted me on my first day), to be my assistant. I told her, "I want you to move your desk right outside of my door. You are my assistant."

Joan was wonderful. I could say to her, "Please send so and so a letter that explains thus and such." She could take my casual verbal notes and convert them to "proper" English and format for me. I didn't have to dictate things out all "proper". She made me look good! She was organized, and kept me organized and going in the right direction.

I was the first guy in the office in the morning, and the last guy to leave. I really knew what was going on with everyone there. My boss wanted me to join Rolling Green Golf Course. I said "no."

Instead of two martini lunches, I would play squash!

Joan Colton

One day, a couple came in to speak with me about their insurance. They showed up about 11 a.m. without an appointment. When my secretary came into the office to tell me they were here, I was concerned that we might have missed or forgotten an appointment. The couple assured me that they had just stopped by without an appointment. "Well," I said, "would you be able to come back later this afternoon? I have a court date at 11:30."

They assured me that they could come back later and we set a time. I, of course, headed to the SQUASH court, while they assumed that I had meant a court of law! When we met that afternoon, they asked me how it had gone. "Fine," I replied. Of course, I knew that I had played a squash game, rather than a court battle!

The president of General Accident Insurance, Ed Leopold, and me on the squash court. (One day, Ed had to go back to the office early from our squash game because someone was coming in to paint his portrait!)

MOM AND DAD

My father's tuberculosis had relapsed in 1959. He had to be treated often, so I took him from one doctor's appointment to another. Dad ended up in a sanitarium in Eagleville, Pa.

Eventually, his doctor said to him, "Peter, if you want to live longer, you have to move back to Italy where the air is cleaner and the living is healthier." They discussed it and in 1964, they moved back to Ferentino. When they went back, they used the same steamer trunk that we'd used on our way over in 1948!

The only photograph of the Cocco's men together – Dad,
me, Leandro, and Americo.

My mother, Barbara, and me – back in Italy.

**My parents' headstone – Pietro Cocco and Barbara
Celani, and a closer look at my father.**

My father lived until March 13, 1971.

In 1974 or 1975, Americo called me out of the blue and invited
me to lunch. I was pleased. I was doing pretty well in life. By
now, I was the district manager for John Hancock. I was making
a good living. All in all, I felt good about myself. Americo was
doing very well. His company, Accurate Tool and Die was
growing by leaps and bounds. I thought that something was up.
Calling me to meet him just wasn't his style.

We met for lunch.

Americo claimed that he'd cried when he heard that I made district manager. I wasn't really buying that. Then he said, "I have something to tell you."

"What is it?"

"Well, when Mom and Dad went back to Italy, they gave me $8,000 to split with you."

"And why didn't you?" I asked.

"I was afraid you'd blow it."

"That wouldn't be any of your business, Americo," I replied. "If you can prove to me that the money is in the bank in an account where my kids will benefit if I die, then all is forgiven."

Of course, he couldn't. He tried to give me the check.

I continued, "In 1964, $4000 was a lot of money. It was almost five month's wages. Now, I make that much in two and a half weeks! I needed the money – desperately – back then. I don't need it now. I needed it when I asked you to pay me $200/week instead of $125/week and you wouldn't, but my barber would lend me $500. Your apologies and explanations are too late."

Had he told me about the $4000 back then, I would have been very grateful. More than grateful. In fact, I probably would have kissed his butt!

"The only reason that you're telling me this now is that your wife, a deeply religious woman, wanted you to do it. Go home and tell her that you gave me the money and that all is forgiven. She'll feel better, but you'll have to live with it."

In retrospect, with a lot of years in the rearview mirror, I realize that Americo refusing to give me the job at $200/week when we were on strike was the best thing that could have happened to me. The very BEST THING. I had to go out and succeed on my own...not in Americo's shadow.

Americo had become wildly successful with Accurate Tool Company. He and Frank had gone their separate ways. Frank opened another place somewhere in Paoli, but Americo went to West Chester and built a place of his own at 891 Fern Hill Road – the location it still occupies today. Americo had all kinds of clients: Mitsubishi, Boeing, Siemens, etc. He even built a place in Mexico to service his clients who manufactured there.

THE DAYS OF WINE AND ROSES

The guy who had just left Philly as district manager and moved to the Media office called me one day. His name was Russ Miller.

"Congratulations," Russ said to me the first time we spoke.

"Thanks," I said, "The Media office is a good office, you'll like it there."

"How about you stop by my house for a drink?" asked Russ.

The "Big Guy" and the "Little Guy".

It turns out that that "drink" was one of the most important introductions I would ever have because Russ and I became very close friends. Meeting Russ Miller was the start of the period that I think of as "The Days of Wine and Roses." Sara had been raising our family, and I'd been working on making a living. We hadn't had a lot of time to form a big group of friends outside of our family. All that changed when I met Russ.

Russ Miller at my retirement party.

The first night that I met Jean, Russ' wife, I had stopped by his house to invite them over to our house later that evening. I was having my second gin martini out of a huge glass (it was really a bucket!) with a giant "M" engraved on it. I wasn't a big drinker, so by now, I was feeling the alcohol. Jean, Russ' wife, came in, sort of "down" because she had had a terrible day. She had been stopped by the cops, but managed to talk herself out of a ticket. As she was talking, I piped up, "Mrs. Miller, I don't want to hear about your problems. I have enough of my own!" I followed that up with, "Of course, Jean, I'm only kidding. I'm sorry if I offended you."

Well.

Imagine my saying that to her the very first time we met? She didn't know that I can be very sarcastic at times! I really wasn't being rude, I was trying to be funny.

I left shortly after that, to go home to get ready to entertain. After I left, Russ said to his wife, "We're going over to Andy's tonight."

"You're kidding me? To that guy's house?"

Believe it or not, we became fast friends. Russ, his wife and their family became an extension of our family.

At this point in our lives, our kids were older. We weren't really drinkers and we didn't have a wide array of friends to socialize with. Through the Millers, we met a bunch of other people, among them the DeMatteo's, the Bucci's, the Humbert's and others. We started having parties and going to parties. Our circle of friends grew and grew.

Russ was a party guy. We'd have cocktails and dinner at the house, then Jean would head home. Russ and I would go to Perkins for pancakes at 2 a.m.! We'd get together one or two times a week for a period of 15 to 20 years. We even had booze brought in from Maryland.

One day, I was in line at the register at ACME, and I hear Russ behind me. "Hey, we're going to a barbeque."

Jean and Russ Miller

The Duffy's, Panestri's and Vetaboli's.

Butch and Louise Ara.

Louise and Butch Ara with Sara.
George Kozer and me in Florida.

Sara with Roy Branton and his wife. Dick
Giacomucci.

Bucci and me (check out the hat!).

"Where?" I ask.

"Your house," he replied. It was just like that. We could invite ourselves over. We would make ourselves part of each other's lives.

As we settled into this new lifestyle, one where we had some money to spend, and friends to visit with all the time. I bought a brand new, 1974 Ford Thunderbird for $8,000! Actually, I have Russ to "blame" for that. He kept pushing me and pressuring me to buy it. Finally, I caved in and bought the car.

One day, after we'd known each other for a while, Russ asked me, "What do you want to do with your life?"

"I want to retire owing the bank $3 million dollars."

Russ looked at me, cocked is head, and said, "Why?"

"Because if I owe the bank $3 million dollars, then I must be worth a whole heck of a lot more!"

When I look back on it, I more than achieved that goal!

Russ died about five years ago. Jean is about 90 and still going strong. We still get together with Jean once and a while.

Tom and Eleanor DiFulvio

Henry Matteo, me, John Grosses and Russ Miller.

Bill, me, and George Kozer.

Sara and me with Harry Marrone and Bobbi Israel.

Optimist Club golf outing.

Mrs. Giacomucci, Betty Lazzari, Mrs. Grosses.

Betty Lazzari, Mrs. Grosses and Mama Bucci.

Ray and Shirley Santucci

Domenic Pennestri (on right)

Sara with Eleanor DiFulvio.

I worked – a lot – but I made a deal with Sara that we would travel. We would go away two or three times a year, once on a trip somewhere within the US, and a second trip to Europe. We went on cruises in the Baltic (and other places), and we skied in Europe. We really enjoyed seeing the world.

One memorable cross-country trip was one we took by train. We left Philadelphia, went through Chicago and stopped in Montana on the way to Washington State. We were supposed to pull into a stop in Montana at a certain time. Sara and I were getting off the train there, and we were going to spend a few days exploring Glacier National Park.

The train's arrival at the station in Montana was delayed by several hours because some other train got the right-of-way over our train. We arrived at midnight. The train dropped us off and pulled out of the station – and then there was nothing. It was pitch black. It was eerily quiet. No lights anywhere. No people anywhere.

Sara was scared to death. I wasn't real happy, but after my eyes adjusted a little bit, I saw a light flickering about 200 yards away. We gathered our bags, and picked our way across to the light. It was hard going because we couldn't see a thing. And, there were bears. We didn't see any, but we knew they were around.

When we arrived at the light, there was an envelope beneath it that said, "Mr. Cocco" on it with a note that said, "Inside is the key to Cabin 32." Miraculously, we'd found our hotel! We didn't know where Cabin 32 was, but we'd walk up to each cabin, check out the number by the door, then move on until we found number 32.

Once inside, the place was lovely. When the sun came up the next morning, we found that the area was the most beautiful we'd seen. We were about a half mile from a campground loaded with travelers. In town, there was an old-fashioned diner that served terrific food. We had a ball!

"Cabin 32" in Montana.

REAL ESTATE

I also started dabbling in real estate. I had some money now, and I wanted to invest it in property. The 1970's had a terrific investment called a Limited Partnership for people who wanted to try to save money on taxes. I bought a share of the Society Hill Club Limited Partnership for $50,000. With that investment came a free, full membership to the club. I could play squash every day! Jefferson Hospital came along in 1987 or 1988 and bought the Club. I got back $48,000 in cash, but by that time, I'd probably gotten $300,000 in tax deductions – not to mention my free membership all those years!

I also bought a condo at 5th and Locust for $108,000. It was a high-rise and the condo was on the 22nd floor overlooking Washington Square Park. I rented that unit out, and had my first income-producing property. In 1988 or 1989, the tenant left. I thought that it might be a nice place for Sara and I to live, so I took her down to see it. She quickly declared, "I won't live down here," so I put it up for sale. A week or two after it was listed, the realtor called me up to tell me that he had an offer for $205,000!

Not bad!

My buddies, Matteo and Bucci, and I actually formed a partnership called "MBC". Together, we bought ground on Route 9 in southern New Jersey. It was a driving range and nursery, but because it had a shed on it, I could mortgage it because it was "developed". We bought the land for $65,000. I wanted us each to set $200/month aside, so that we could buy more property, but the guys were giddy with making money on this property and didn't want to go for more.

A few months after we bought it, we were offered $80,000 for the land. "M" and "B" wanted to sell, but "C" did not. I just knew that this was the time to be BUYING, not to be selling. The people who wanted to buy the property really wanted it, and eventually, they offered us $125,000 for it. "M" and "B" forced my hand, and we had to sell. After the closing, we went to Cape May to celebrate the sale, but I wasn't in a celebrating mood...I still thought we should have held onto it, and bought more.

That was the last time that I had any partners in my real estate purchases. As good of friends as Matteo and Bucci were, we had different investment strategies, and I didn't want to lose the friendships over business.

Henry Matteo, Russ Miller and me.

LAKE CHAMPLAIN

One of the places that Sara really wanted to go to was Montreal. In 1981, we spent a few days up on Lake George in New York. Sara didn't know it, but I was planning on taking her up to Montreal. We enjoyed Lake George, and when we left, I took Route 9 instead of the highway, I-87. We headed towards Lake Champlain, planning on continuing up the lake to Montreal. As we were driving through Wheelsboro, N.Y., we spotted a real estate office. Sara said, "Why don't you stop in and see what's going on up here?"

I went in and chatted with the real estate agent that was there that day. I asked him about the difference between Lake George (mostly vacation homes) and Lake Champlain (more permanent residences). He asked if we'd like to see a couple of lots, and off we went.

I didn't like the first lot that we looked at, but the guy had another one 'up his sleeve'. He took us to the second lot, and it was absolutely beautiful. The lot sat right on Lake Champlain...right on the water. The cost: $18,000.

I told him that I'd buy it if I had the money. When he said that they could finance it, I was sold. I put $1,000 down on the lot and off we headed to Montreal (which was, after all, the point of the drive).

When we were heading back home, we stopped back in Wheelsboro to finalize the deal. I wanted to stop by the lot first, but I'd actually forgotten how to find it. I had to ask the realtor for directions again. That was a little bit embarrassing!

I asked him if there was any way we could put a prefab cabin on the lot. The guy directed me to a lumberyard. They had prefabbed units for sale. When I asked who could actually put it on the lot, they directed me to Leon Lemoy. We met Leon in the supermarket parking lot in Keesville. He said that it would cost $10,000-$15,000 to put the cabin on the lot, but for a little bit more, he could build a custom three-bedroom place with a garage and a porch. We were sold!

The house grew over the years. In the end, it was a pretty terrific place!

We made a bunch of new friends up there, and took up a whole bunch of hobbies that were new to us. We started fishing, boating, ice fishing, snowmobiling, duck hunting, skiing and frog shooting ("frog shooting" is where you shoot frogs off a lily pad with a .22. You take off their legs and have frog legs for dinner! We used to get enough frog legs to fill a 5-gallon tub). At one point, we had four boats: a 26-foot boat, a rowboat to get to the 26-foot boat, a canoe, and a wave runner!

The water in the lake is always cold – so cold that you have to wear a wetsuit year-round.

The lake freezes over – solidly – every winter. We could actually drive across it to pull our fishing shacks out to our holes.

Because the lake froze, you'd have to pull your dock out of the water before winter set in. If you didn't, the dock would be damaged by the force of the ice.

On our newly poured foundation.

Cocco's, Matteo's and Miller's standing in the construction zone.

The best view of the house was from the lake.

Our boat anchored in Lake Champlain.

You kept in shape climbing the stairs!

The Matteo's and Shelmerdine's at the lake.

More friends at Lake Champlain.

Fishing shacks.

Toboggan on the lake behind the snowmobile.

Brian Bareby and me.

Bud Humbert with two fishing poles through the ice.

Duck hunting with Tanner.

On the deck with a cocktail.

Canoeing with our neighbor's son, Tanner (a few years
earlier than the hunting shot).

We'd go up to Montreal for the evening (it was only an hour drive).

While I was still at John Hancock, after I'd gotten the office running smoothly, I would take 4-day weekends all summer. I'd take Friday and Monday as vacation. Sara would come into the city to meet me on Thursday night, then we'd drive up to Lake Champlain. We'd come back Monday night, and I'd be at the office bright and early on Tuesday morning.

I worked hard to make sure that the office was running smoothly, but now that it was, it was my time to party, as well. This whole time was a party...almost from the day I first met Russ. I was working, but I was also vacationing, investing in real estate, skiing, traveling cross-country by train, visiting Canada, touring Europe, etc. It was a wonderful time!

THE 1970's CONTINUE

As I continued on in my role as district manager, my family was growing up and moving on with their lives. I felt that I owed all of my kids the education that I never got. I told each of them, "I owe you an education, but you're not going away to school. You'll sleep at home. There's nothing you can learn anywhere else that you can't learn in Philly."

Andy (not a 'Junior' because he is 'Andrew Joseph' after Sara's father) went to pharmacy school and is still a pharmacist.

Linda went to St. Joe's and works at DuPont in IT. She's been very successful.

Lisa went to hairdressing school, then ultimately, became a nurse. I wanted to buy her a salon down on MacDade Avenue, but she said "no.". She wanted a change and is a terrific nurse.

Our kids - Mike, Linda, Andy and Lisa.

Andy's wedding in 1980 with me and Mike.

My daughters, Lisa and Linda.

Mike decided that he didn't want to go to college. That was fine with me (after all, I'd done OK and I hadn't even finished 5th grade), but I told him to find something he wanted to do, so that he didn't have to work for anyone else. I just didn't want someone taking advantage of him because he was a hard worker.

While he was still in high school, Mike started working at Pepe's Pizza owned by Spiro. He worked hard and liked the business. In 1978, Mike came to me and said that Spiro wanted to sell. I asked Mike to show me what it was doing...how he could make it work, and he did. Mike was just a kid and he'd already saved $7,000-$8,000, so he was doing pretty well.

Mike asked me to see if we could make a deal with Spiro. I met Spiro at the Lantern on Oak Avenue. "I heard you want to sell," I said, "My son wants me to talk to you about buying. What do you want for it?"

We chatted, and I found out that he wanted $175,000 for the building and the shop, and that he would hold the mortgage. Interest rates at the time were 10-14%, so they weren't exactly 'cheap'. I thought that that sounded like too much for what he was offering. I told Spiro that I'd pay for the beer, but we weren't going to buy the place. He said to me, "How much would you pay?" I believe that people shouldn't play games, so I just answered, "Nothing. We're done." I told Michael that we weren't buying Pepe's. He got really pissed-off at me because he'd wanted me to make the deal.

While I'm not great at reading and writing, I'm really pretty good with numbers. I realized that the $175,000 price at a 10-12% interest rate wasn't going to allow anyone to make a profit, so I wasn't going to make the deal. Mike was mad, but I told him to leave it up to me. I'd find something.

I checked with a realtor friend of mine, and found out that #1 Chester Pike in Norwood was for sale for $35,000. It was just three-quarters of a mile down the road from Pepe's. That was more like it! I went and looked at the place and I thought it would work as a pizza place.

I told Mike that if he wanted to go into the pizza business, fine, but that we weren't paying $175,000 for Spiro's place. We could buy our own shop for $35,000 and go from there. I said to Mike, "Go and offer $35,000 for the place. Don't go in at $32,000, play a bunch of games, then risk losing it. $35,000 is a fair price. Just go in and offer the full amount."

We got the building. I was in the real estate business, and Mike was in the pizza business. He didn't have a mortgage. He didn't report to anyone (other than me!) and he didn't owe anyone anything.

I had a condo in Brigantine, N.J., so I spent time there. I liked the pizza that I had at The Castle in Brigantine. Walt Gouta owned The Castle (he now owns Primos Pizza on the Ocean City Boardwalk). I told Walt that I thought his pizza was good and wondered if I could have his recipe.

"Sure, come in and I'll show you. If you need help setting it up, I'll show you how to do it." Walt was willing to help us in any way he could. The Cocco's pizza recipe started as Walt Gouta's.

What I didn't know was that Mike really knew NOTHING about the pizza business!!! He could make a good pizza, but that was about it.

The first day he's in business Mike calls me up, "Pop, the pizzas won't cook right." We came to find out that the ovens that were in the place weren't pizza ovens, they were bakers ovens. We could make a mean roll, but we couldn't cook a pizza properly. We needed pizza ovens!

It is late June. We've just opened up. The ovens are the wrong ovens. I'm leaving for Italy the next week. We've got a problem.

I knew that there was a restaurant equipment supply shop at 3rd and Market. I was one block away in my John Hancock office. I left my office, and went right to the supply house. I told them that I needed pizza ovens and I needed them right away. They told me they didn't have any. I saw something sitting on the other side of the warehouse that looked suspiciously like a pizza oven.

"What's that," I asked?

"That's a pizza oven, but it's going to Reading."

"No, they're going to Norwood."

"No, they're going to Reading."

...and so it went.

Finally, I said, "Look, I have a problem. There's only one way to correct it, and that's for me to get two new pizza ovens."

"You're not getting those ovens," said the guy. "Even if I sold them to you, it's a holiday week, and you won't get anyone to install them on this short notice."

I had seen another guy walking around in the warehouse, as we were talking. I called over to him, "Hey, do you set up pizza ovens?"

"Yes," he replied, "That's my job."

"How much do you normally make a day?" I asked.

He responded, "About $100."

"I'll give you $600 to set these two pizza ovens up in Norwood. I'll pay cash for the ovens, and to you to install them."

They installed them the day before we left for Italy.

Mike was in business.

As things moved along, we found that the mixers kept breaking. I went back to my restaurant supplier and asked him what we needed. He showed me that I needed this and this and this.

"Why didn't you tell me that I needed these?"

"Why didn't you ask?"

"I'm asking now!"

He told me all the things that we should have had to properly equip a pizza shop. I bought those things, got them installed, and Norwood was under way.

Original Cocco's Menu

THE 1980's

I was doing pretty well, myself. I had one of John Hancock's most successful offices. Bill Rhodes, one of the "bigwigs" from Boston (John Hancock's headquarters) tried to get me to go to school. "You're a district manager, you need a CLU," he said. The CLU was an insurance certification.

"Listen," I said, "I know my product. That's what's important. Every time you come out with a new policy, I buy it myself, because I want to know how it works. I know what works and what doesn't. I don't need more letters behind my name to do my job."

Me in my office at 325 Chestnut Street, Philly.

At one point, there were 200 offices in the country. There were all kinds of meetings. Meetings in Philadelphia, meetings in Boston, meetings other places. I'd play squash with some of the upper-level managers and we'd have a ball, but when I had to deal with them off the squash court or out of the office, I felt out of place.

I'd travel to Boston fairly frequently for meetings with the executives – the president of John Hancock and other big shots. At lunchtime, we'd all go to the Executive Dining Room for our meal. Everything was fancy tableware and fine linens. When we got in these kind of settings, I got very uncomfortable. I felt like I didn't have the language to have conversations with these guys. I'd get so nervous that my palms would sweat, and I couldn't eat a thing.

After struggling through a few of these lunches, I finally asked my boss if it would be OK for me to go down and eat in the employee cafeteria. "Really?" he wanted to know.

"Absolutely."

"OK. If that's what you want." He was incredulous. I went off to the cafeteria a happy man.

After I did it the first day, I asked him, "Can I eat down there every day?"

"Sure," he replied, shaking his head.

I felt that things were going the wrong way for John Hancock. I watched and I read about the products. They weren't paying attention to their core business…they kept adding different business lines, but many of them didn't make money, and they couldn't control it correctly.

Later in the 1980's, I was talking to Mr. Rhodes. I told him that the company was going in the wrong direction. We were now selling car insurance, homeowners, property and casualty, long-term care, mutual funds, disability, as well as, the bread and butter, life insurance. Many of those products just couldn't be sold at a profit in certain areas, so people were lying on applications in order to make the sale.

For example, if we entered the correct zip code on a property and casualty application for South Philly, it would be denied. However, if a salesman from Upper Darby entered the zip code for the Upper Darby office for a house that was actually in South Philly, then the application would be approved. This was before computers. No one was double-checking things to make sure that the information on the applications was really accurate before they made the approval. Of course, that meant that there was a good likelihood that John Hancock was going to lose money on that policy.

Here's another example of places that John Hancock would lose money:

Profesco, Regional Director.

When all the self-storage units began springing up, John Hancock formed a division, Profesco, to sell the insurance on the units. Here was a totally different type of insurance that we had to service. It even required me to carry a separate business card. I was still the District Manager for John Hancock, but I was ALSO a "regional director" at Profesco.

Every type of insurance required a different license, so my guys were always applying for new licenses. Every license application needed to be notarized. Rather than having everyone running all over the city looking for a notary, I decided to apply to be a notary myself. Problem solved!

As the 1980's progressed, I was getting fed up in the insurance business. The world was changing. Interest rates were at 21%! I thought the world had gone crazy!

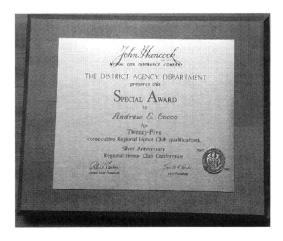

25 consecutive Regional Honor Club awards – 1960-1985. I'm not sure that I've ever seen anyone else receive this award!

I felt that I'd done about everything that I could do in my John Hancock career. I had started dabbling in real estate and found that I liked it. That was to become the next chapter in my life! Starting in 1982, I began making my plans to get out of John Hancock for good.

My 50th Birthday Party - Me, Bob Bucci and John Grosses.

Sara and me with Joe Corsins and his wife.

On the right, Bob Bucci.

Ron Tassoni, Dick Giacomucci and Gino Lazzari.

Me with Betty and John Grosses (and Sara peeking out on the right).

COCCO'S PIZZA ON OAK AVENUE IS BORN

Mike had been operating Norwood for a year, or a year and a half, when he decided that he wanted a second location. We found it at 540 Oak Avenue, Primos, Pa. in the building which housed Paul's Diner.

We rented the building and opened our second Cocco's Pizza.

Next door, at 550 Oak Avenue, What's the Scoop (an ice cream place) was always busy. Their lot would be overflowing. The parking lot at 540 Oak Avenue was full, but I would look in, and Cocco's would be empty. All those cars were for the place next door! Why?

I looked around and walked up and down the street. There it was staring me in the face. The place just wasn't inviting. I wouldn't stop in there to buy anything, either. The building needed some serious work.

I went to the owner, Paul Bedwell, and said, "One of us has got to go." He was ready to retire, so he was motivated to sell. He sold us the whole lot (which included what is now the warehouse, the laundromat and the restaurant) for $275,000 and he held the mortgage.

There were two garages in the back, in addition to the restaurant.

We started designing a whole new set of buildings...the new restaurant, as well as, some other spaces in what is the warehouse today. We got the plans approved, and the bank agreed to lend us the money.

We kept the tenants in the back because it provided us with some cash flow. We started building the new restaurant next to the old one. The cost of the new development? $500,000.

In 1982, interest rates were 20-21% (gulp!). I'd worked hard to develop a good relationship with the loan officer at IVB Bank. He knew what we wanted to do, and was willing to lend us the money to make it happen. He saw the plans for the shop, and told me, "You keep building. I'll give you the money as you need it." We were a good way through and had about $100,000 left to draw on the loan, when the unthinkable happened. Our loan officer left the bank. When the new loan officer, Carol Stella, came in to see what we were up to, I showed her the plans, showed her around the construction, and figured everything was all A-OK. She left, but called me back a day or two later. "They don't want to let you have the additional funding."

"But I need it to finished," I replied. "I was told that I could keep drawing as I needed it, up to another $100,000."

"No," was all that she had to say.

I went to Americo and asked him if I could use $50,000 of his rather considerable line of credit. "I can make the payments with no problem, and I'll pay you the interest."

The new restaurant rises on the right, while the old place is torn down on the left.

Americo said, "You know a lot of banks and a lot of people. I can't do it. Go get the money from one of them." Again, my brother wasn't going to support what I wanted to do.

I was going broke with a half completed building...and I've got to tell you, I was worried.

John Hancock was at 4th and Chestnut. IVB Bank was at 18th and Market. I called IVB Bank and told the person who answered the phone that I needed to speak with the president. When his secretary answered, she asked me what I needed to speak to him about. I told her that the bank was about to lose $400,000. She tried to get more information out of me, but that was all that I would say. I told her, "You just give him that message, then have him call me back."

Sure enough, about five minutes later, the secretary called me back. "Please hold for the president."

When she connected me, I said, "Your bank is about to lose $400,000, but if you'll give me 15 minutes of time, you can save it. I can be there in 15 minutes." He told me to come on over.

I left my office with the blueprints under my arm and made a beeline for the bank. When I got into the president's office, I unrolled the prints on the coffee table in the president's office. The blueprints were all stamped as "approved" from Harrisburg, which proved that they had passed all of the requirements for zoning and the like.

I explained to him what we are doing. This is how far we've gotten in the process. "I need $100,000 to finish the project (which had been authorized by my last banker), but now I am told that 'they' won't give me the money. I want to know who 'they' are. Just 'who' is 'they'?"

The president of IVB picked up his phone, mumbled something, and soon a number of 'they' came into the office (including Carol Stella), lined up in front of him. "Who said that Mr. Cocco couldn't have the $100,000?" he asked them.

There was some mumbling, and shuffling of feet. The president looked them over, then declared, "Give him the money."

He looked at me and said, "I think you're good for it."

540 Oak Avenue – Completed!

We had enough to complete the building, and I didn't need my brother. I had done it on my own!

We had a video store, flower shop, bakery, and Marty's Garage in the back. We rented them cheap to make sure that they stayed rented, so that we had that income to count on.

I told my family, "One day all of these buildings will be Cocco's." As we paid down the $500,000 loan, we let the leases expire, and we'd take over the space. Marty's Garage was the last one out. The entire property is now Cocco's!

MOM'S DEATH

I was on my way out of the house one day in the fall of 1986, when my daughter, Lisa, came running down the stairs saying that Aunt Eleanor (Americo's wife) was on the phone. When I picked it up, Eleanor told me that my mother was sick and in a coma. She was close to death.

My mother, Barbara and me, when she was about 80-years old.

"Let me speak to my brother," I asked.

"He's already in Italy," replied my sister-in-law.

WHAT!?!?!?

I dialed my mother's in Italy and who should answer the phone, but Americo.

"Why didn't you call me before you left?"

"I was in a hurry."

"You mean, there wasn't time between learning that Mom was gravely ill, to getting on the plane to spare a minute to call your brother? Never mind, pick me up when I get in."

Americo declared that he couldn't do that because he could never live with himself if he left to pick me up and Mom passed while he was gone. Then, I asked him to have one of my nephews, Massimo or Pietro, pick me up.

"Leave them alone," was Americo's response.

I hung up, made my reservation, flew to Italy, rented a car, and got out to Ferentino before mom died.

Americo's return ticket was scheduled for two or three days from my arrival. We were standing by the bed, and being the sarcastic guy that I can be, I said to my mother (remember, she's in a coma), "Mom, I know you can't hear me, but your son's ticket home is going to expire in two or three days, so you'd better get well or die, otherwise, he'll be stuck."

Mom lasted a few more days, but on November 2, 1986, she passed away.

Mom in her kitchen.

My mother was truly a wonderful woman. Her life had not been easy. My father had all but abandoned her and the family when he went to the United States in 1922. He came back occasionally, and sent money occasionally, but she had to deal with day-to-day life on her own. It wasn't easy. She had to raise three boys on her own. She had to deal with the sharecroppers, the Nazis, the Moroccans, the work, and the hunger during the war on her own. True, she had family around her, but that's not the same as facing the world with your husband.

My father had to have been aware of what was going on in the world in the late 1930's. He should have sent for his family then and brought us to the United States before the war. Instead, my mother had to play the cards that she was dealt.

Through it all, I never once heard my mother complain. She was an amazing woman.

**Headstone engraving of my mother,
Barbara Celani.**

Pietro Cocco and Barbara Celani Cocco Crypt.

When we were in Italy for this last visit with Mom, I asked Americo to switch his ticket home to match when I was flying back. I figured that that would give us time to talk, time to figure out what the heck was going on with him. I wanted to know what I had done to make him so angry with me.

Americo wouldn't do it. He was going to fly back when he was going to fly back.

I said, "I could write a book on what I've done for you."

I continued with, "I'll give you two weeks for you to tell me ONE thing that you've done for me. If I don't hear from you, we're done."

I never heard from him, and we lost touch for many, many years. It was sad because my kids also lost their relationship with their cousins during that time. It hurt everyone in the family, not just me.

Leandro, Massimo, Mom and me.

RETIREMENT FROM JOHN HANCOCK

I was 55 ½ and I was DONE with the insurance business. It had been good to me, but I wanted out. The whole time I was district manager in Philly, there hadn't been one work stoppage. We had been a productive office. We'd made a lot of money for John

Hancock.

At one point, my regional manager said to me, "You've got to forget making pizza, you have a job to do."

My reply was simply, "I've never made a pizza in my life." He just didn't understand, and I wasn't going to try to explain it.

As things continued to spiral downward in the insurance industry, I saw the writing on the wall. I knew that there were going to be consolidations. I knew they were going to start shuttering offices. When I was ready to leave, I offered my office as one of the first to be closed down.

I retired in 1989. In all the time I was district manager, I never had a grievance filed against the office with the union. To this day, I'm proud of that record.

They threw me a terrific retirement party. Everyone came and said kind words (and, of course, sort of "roasted" me). I was going to miss some of the people, but I wasn't going to miss the direction that the insurance industry was heading.

I might have retired from John Hancock when I was young, but I certainly wasn't done! In addition to the golf, real estate investing and traveling, I did things like woodworking. Each of my grandkids got a handmade rocking horse! The saddle was made with genuine leather, and the mane/tail from real hair. A couple even had real stirrups!

We sold the house up on Lake Champlain around 2001/2002, and started spending more time at the shore, Ventnor, to be exact.

My retirement party – *Newsweek* and "Man of the Week" mock-up.

I moved my office (desk, chairs and all) to my house –
here are the awards as they hang on my wall
today...don't forget to check out the hole-in-one shots!

One of the rocking horses.

Mike's kids – Michele, Michael and Matt.

I also made train mailboxes! Mine is still in use today.

Train mailboxes – mine was the Papà train, of course!

How about this blanket rack (in front of my 'world' wallpaper where I've pinned all the states/countries I've visited).

My last boat, out on the bay in Ventnor.

UNCLE LUIGI

Uncle Luigi remained in Ferentino, and lived until 1991, far outliving my father.

He had been kind to me when my father was in the United States and I was still living in Ferentino. He wasn't a warm and fuzzy person, but he made sure that I was OK. If I needed something, he made sure that I had it.

On one of my trips back to Italy, after Uncle Luigi had had a stomach operation, we took a ride up into the mountains, just the two of us. Uncle Luigi knew that I love goat meat, and he knew that up in the mountains were the best restaurants that served it. Because he'd had a stomach operation, he couldn't eat well, so I got to eat both his portion and mine! We had a nice time.

Uncle Luigi and Aunt Victoria's headstone.

REUNITED WITH AMERICO

Sometime in 2001 or 2002, I was in Gentile's Market on Route 252 in Newtown Square. Lo and behold, I see Americo in front of me. I was shocked at how he had aged.

"Hello, old man," I said to him. When he turned around and saw me, he grabbed me in a huge hug and wouldn't let me go.

"You've missed so much, Americo. You've missed so much."

We re-established our relationship and he couldn't do enough for me. Unfortunately, there was nothing that he could do to recapture the lost time. He was extremely successful, but he wasn't a happy man.

Americo and me in Italy.

We played some golf together (he'd gotten A LOT better!). We traveled some together. We went to Italy – back home. Sara, Eleanor, Americo, and I took a car trip to Disney World.

Unfortunately, Americo didn't live in the moment, he was always looking to the next moment, so that he didn't relax and enjoy the ride and the travel (literally and figuratively).

That was OK though. In hindsight, he'd given me the greatest gift by refusing to lend me that money when I needed it. My life went on an entirely different – and wonderful – path. Americo and I made our peace. We were brothers again. Our families were able to get to know one another. The cousins could re-establish their relationships and friendships.

Our two family together after many years.

My daughter-in-law, Theresa, Mike's wife, with America's daughter Barbara.

America was very ill by the time we got back together, but we had some good days. We'd missed a lot of time together, but we ended up on a high note. We made things "right".

UNCLE ALFREDO'S FAMILY

My dad's brother, Alfredo, had been in the U.S., in Brooklyn, before my dad arrived. He had three kids, Mary, Lena and Pasquale (named after my grandfather).

Mary grew up and married Joe, and auto mechanic. They had two boys, Joe and Donald, both of whom became NYC police officers (NYPD). Joe was injured in the line of duty. Donald is retired and is now a chauffeur for some bigwig in New York.

Lena was the most beautiful woman that I ever laid eyes on. When she was around, I couldn't take my eyes off of her! Lena married an attorney, but he didn't like her to associate with my family because we were 'beneath' them. Their son actually came down to see me in Secane. He said, "I should have come sooner, I didn't know I had such a nice and welcoming family."

Alfredo's daughter, my cousin, Mary Cocco in New York City.

SOME THOUGHTS ON LEANDRO

My brother, Leandro, is 11 years older than me. He was already living away from home when I was young, so I didn't really get to know him them. I rarely saw him, but by the time I was studying at the seminary, he became the person who watched after me closely. He became a father figure to me. My dad hadn't been around when I was growing up, so we never had a close relationship. Leandro, who was very kind to me, stepped in and filled that role. He taught me to be "a man". Like me, his word was his bond. If he told you he was going to do something, you could be sure that he would do it.

A painting done of my brother Leandro and me (I'm on the left) outside of his house in Italy.

I owe everything I am to Leandro. He taught me. He encouraged me in everything that I did. I went back to Italy to visit him every year because I loved him so much.

If I added all the time I spent with my father, in the same house, it added up to maybe one year. I called him "Papà", but I never had the feeling of "Papà" in my heart. Instead, Leandro holds the place of "Papà" in my heart.

Leandro would sit for hours in front of his house, back in Ferentino, reading the paper cover-to-cover, doing a book of crossword puzzles a week (he'd send the completed books in and actually won prizes). As he got older, and couldn't walk well, we'd sit in front of the house talking and telling stories.

Leandro and me during one of my visits.

Leandro, his son Dr. Peter, and me.

Leandro and Anna's 50th wedding anniversary.

Lisa, me, Flavio, Catia, Anna and Leandro.

Pietro, Leandro, Massimo, and me at Massimo's daughter's (Emanuela) wedding in 2011.

Leandro's 90th birthday party in 2012.

Leandro's headstone image and Anna, his wife.

PRINCESS RYE

Princess Rye was a wonderful lady, a lady that I adored...and Sara wasn't even jealous!

Back then, I-95 through Philadelphia wasn't complete, so I'd drive the back road to work – down Oak Avenue and up through Essington. Down Oak Lane there was a sign company called Lane Signs. Lane Signs did all of the signs for Cocco's. Unfortunately, the guy who owned the business also liked to play the horses, so he needed money – often. One day I stopped in on my way to or from work, and he said that he had to sell the business because he needed money. I decided to buy the business, but before I did, I asked, "Does the horse go with it?"

"Yes", was the answer. Enter Princess Rye into my life.

Princess Rye

Me, Princess Rye and Sara. (I put us in order, left-to-right, just to be sure you would know who was who!)

With ownership came privileges. I even got an "owner's card" to the track.

Princess Rye stood 17 hands tall (that's 5'8"at the withers – the top of her shoulders). We owned her for a couple of years, and she lived near, and raced at, Philadelphia Park.

When I first got her, I had a little talk with Princess Rye. "As long as you earn your keep, I'll stick with you."

She did pretty well on the track and managed to earn her keep, as the saying goes, but we never earned back the initial investment of $20,000. Unfortunately, she got hurt, so I decided that I would give her to the vet that had been taking care of her. She got to retire "in style".

TRAVELING FAR AND WIDE

When I first started earning "real money" at John Hancock, Sara and I began to travel – both in the U.S. and outside. Later, after

I retired, we traveled even more extensively. We traveled the world, and had great adventures all along the way. We traveled by car and train and plane and boat! If there was an adventure to be had, we went on it!

I wanted all of my grandkids to know Ferentino and Italy, so I tried to take them over when they got old enough to appreciate it. I think that I took six of them over.

Michelle and Drew again.

We wanted to see this great country of ours, but we also wanted to see the world. Along the way, we visited 32 states:

Alabama	Indiana	North Dakota
Arizona	Louisiana	Ohio
California	Maine	Oklahoma
Colorado	Maryland	Pennsylvania

Connecticut	Massachusetts	Puerto Rico
Delaware	Montana	South Carolina
Florida	Nevada	Texas
Georgia	New Jersey	Vermont
Hawaii	New Mexico	Virginia
Idaho	New York	Washington
Illinois	North Carolina	West Virginia

We also saw countries and had experiences all over the world. Among the countries we visited were:

Argentina	Falkland Islands (penguins stink!)	Panama
Armenia	Germany	Peru
Austria	Greece	Poland
Belgium	Guatemala	Portugal
Brazil	Hungary	Romania
Canada	Ireland	Russia
Chile	Israel	San Marino
Costa Rica	Italy (of course!)	Scotland
Cyprus	Latvia	Slovakia
Czechoslovakia	Lithuania	Spain
Denmark	Luxembourg	Sweden
Egypt	Mexico	Switzerland

El Salvador	Monaco	Turkey
England	Morocco	Vatican City
Estonia	Norway	Wales

(check out the photos at the end to see some of the sights!)

COCCO'S PIZZA EXPANDS

As the years went by, more and more "kids", young men who had worked for us at one of the locations, wanted to run a Cocco's Pizza! Mike focused on the flagship location, Primos. We sold the original location, Norwood, to one of the "kids", then bought some other buildings and set these guys on their way. That helped me keep my passion for real estate satisfied AND gave a lot of young men an opportunity to start their own business that they probably never could have done on their own (because it costs a lot of money to open up a pizza shop).

It was a good deal for both of us. We were able to expand Cocco's beyond the limits of our family, and they get to run their business. The only requirement? They have to buy their dough, sauce and cheese from us! That way, the pizza is similar, regardless of which Cocco's someone goes in.

Does the guy in the logo look familiar?!?!

FRANCHISE OPPORTUNITY
COCCO'S PIZZA

FAMOUS COCCO'S PIZZA

Pizza dough and sauce made fresh daily. We use only 100% mozzarella cheese and other wholesome ingredients. Popular pricing. These are the elements that make Cocco's Pizza the favorite for so many enthusiastic customers. It's no wonder. Our delicious pizza is unique, and prepared using our trade secret recipes. We're not only the best; we're one of the biggest in the Philadelphia area. Last year, we sold over 250,000 pizza's to our hungry, satisfied customers, more than any other local pizza retailer. We are operating nine retail shops. As a result of strong demand, we recently decided to franchise our business, and we have had excellent results.

Franchisees buy all their needs for Cocco's Pizza -- dough and sauce -- directly from the company. However, there's never a royalty or ongoing franchise fee.

The cost to open a Cocco's Pizza shop is $60,000.00 or more, depending upon the shop location and the cost of leasehold improvements. Some equipment used in operation of the shop can be leased, ask us for the details.

Our food and beverage products are superb. One taste will convince you as it has convinced our growing army of customers. The Cocco's Pizza franchise opportunity is based upon our products, and a sounder base would be hard to find.

COCCO'S PIZZA
SEVEN-STEP PROGRAM FOR YOUR SUCCESS

1. Cocco's Pizza Beats the Competition.

Although there are many other pizza shops, none of them offers the combination of consistency , taste, wholesome ingredients and quality. Our customers know that with Cocco's Pizza they will have a good, satisfying experience each and every time they visit a Cocco's Pizza shop.

We all want the highest possible return on capital investment in the most productive use of equipment and personnel. The Cocco's system and products can permit you to achieve these results.

2. By Joining Cocco's, You Become Part of a Team.

When you join a franchise group, you eliminate the trials and errors of starting a new business on your own. The kinks have been ironed out through our experience. Right from the start, you benefit from the proven success of others as you participate in a constant, ongoing exchange of information from our corporate headquarters, and from an always-available contact with your fellow franchise owners.

You will be in business for yourself but not by yourself. Help or advice will just be a telephone call away.

3. We Provide a Tested System.

Cocco's has developed and tested a system for operation of shops offering pizza, hoagies, steak sandwiches, snack items and beverages. It would be nice if we could tell you that our past experience has been a flawless one. However, the contrary is true. Mistakes were made; we learned from them. Money was spent in areas that proved unproductive; we noted them. Products were tested, which proved not to meet our standards; we eliminated them. Procedures were tried which didn't work; we instituted new ones. When you purchase a Cocco's Pizza franchise, you save all of the time and aggravation we lived through, and all of the money we spent spotting mistakes and unnecessary expenses.

Our business system is comprehensive, encompassing as you will see everything from initial start-up to product ordering and preparation, from administration to business management. It is a successful system, one that works. When you use it, you learn what we have learned.

4. The Cocco's Pizza Training Program Prepares You To Control The Business With Complete Confidence.

Under our expert guidance, the program is conducted in a structured environment that prepares franchisees for the responsibilities of owning and operating a profitable Cocco's Pizza shop.

The training program brings you to the Cocco's Pizza corporate headquarters. You learn about our products and services, pizza preparation, shop operations and Cocco's policies and procedures. But that's not all. We give you on-the-spot field training at an operational Cocco's Pizza shop. Our training program is comprehensive, yet not complex. We also believe that training does not end the day you open your business. Additional training is available after you open, if needed.

5. **Careful Market and Site Selection Help Determine Your Success Right From The Start.**

No business could succed unless it opens its doors at the right time, and the right place. This has led Cocco's to develop demographic criteria, to identify areas with maximum consumer potential. But determining likely areas is simply not enough.

We know that the specific location of your pizza shop can make a very big difference. We have prepared site selection criteria, which would be made available to you to expedite the search for your location. In addition, we get further involved by actually approving your site, so that you do not get a site which we consider not to be viable.

We are sensitive to the fact that some prospective Cocco's Pizza shop owners want to have a location selected prior to fully committing to a franchise agreement. For this reason, we have developed an option program, which permits you to start the site selection process even prior to signing the franchise agreement. So if you want the assurance of a location before signing on the dotted line, be sure to explore this program.

6. Shop Operation and Support

The Cocco's Pizza management team is composed of able, experienced and hard-working professionals working on your behalf. We are ready, willing and able to spend the time necessary to help your business operate successfully and at peak efficiency. We make available a wide range of services to better enable you to profitably operate a Cocco's Pizza shop. We can help you to maintain the high standards of quality and service which your customer expects and demands.

7. We Provide a Variety of Specialized Services to Our Franchisees.

In order to operate a business such as Cocco's, you must have many skills. We impart these during our training program. And in order to make your success more likely, you must be provided with many services. The Cocco's franchise program takes your needs fully into account. It grants you an exclusive territory in which to operate your shop, establishes a long-term relationship with you to ensure stability, provides you with name identification as "Cocco's Pizza," establishes an image for the business which works to the benefit of all , determines detailed specifications for operation of a Cocco's Pizza shop to ensure quality and uniformity, and gives you access to the propriatary Cocco's Pizza products. When you purchase a Cocco's Pizza franchise, you are purchasing a comprehensive business program and package of services.

COCCO'S PIZZA AN EXCEPTIONAL FRANCHISE OPPORTUNITY

Is it for you?

Since opening our business in 1979, we have built one of the leading pizza and sandwich shop success stories in the Delaware Valley.

The financial potential for Cocco's Pizza franchise owners is impressive. But in return for what can be substantial rewards; franchise owners must be prepared to devote considerable time, effort and financial resources to the business.

Are you able to meet the challanges of this rewarding business? This information should help you decide if a Cocco's Pizza franchise is right for you.

YOUR ESTIMATED INVESTMENT	
The estimated investment to open a Cocco's Pizza shop is as follows:	
Category of Expenses	**Estimated Expense**
License Fee and Set-up	$20,000
Equipment & Installation	$28,700
Signage	$500
Rent & Lease Deposits	$2,500
Leasehold Improvements	$6,000
Miscellaneous	$1,350
Working Capital	$5,000
TOTALS:	$64,050

EVERYTHING YOU RECEIVE

As you see, it's there for the taking. An independent way of life, free from many of the normal risks of self-employment. In summary, our franchise can mean for you:

- Advertising and sales promotion.
- Freedom and independence of your own business.
- Comprehensive training that can put you on top of your business.
- A name and identification for the marketplace.
- Fully developed and operational business system.
- Excellent proprietary products.
- Operational advice and assistance.
- Continual distribution of helpfull information.
- A franchise program gearing our system towards expansion and even greater growth and profits.
- Store design and equipment specifications.

HOW YOU GET STARTED

Since becoming a Cocco's Pizza franchise owner represents an important step, we're sure you'd like to get to know us and the operation first-hand before making a decision. You can start this process in motion by either informing us of your interests or arranging to visit us. Neither of these actions entails any obligation on your part or ours. It merely lets us know of your interest.

You can discuss your future with top management personnel, who will offer guidance and supply answers to your questions. Then, if we are both convinced that it is in your and our best interest to proceed, we can sign a contract and establish a relationship. Financial arrangements will then be made, and your training will be ready to begin at a mutually agreeable time.

So, whether independence to you means financial independence, freedom to come and go as you please, or improved working conditions, you can achieve these goals. Our unique pizza products and franchise program make it possible.

■ Contact:

Daniel Herron
Franchise Sales Director
540 Oak Avenue
Primos, PA 19108
(215) 751-0008 (Day)
&
(215) 543-4266 (Evening)

ALL THE COCCO'S PIZZA SHOPS TODAY

The Original Cocco's – 1 Chester Pike, Norwood, Pa.

540 Oak Avenue, Primos, Pa. – The restaurant.

540 Oak Avenue, Primos, Pa. – The warehouse – Mike, Sr.; Mike, Jr.; Matt; and me.

540 Oak Avenue, Primos, Pa. – Inside the warehouse where we make the dough, rolls, and sauce, and grate the cheese.

Aston, Pa.

Brookhaven, Pa.

Downingtown, Pa.

Drexel Hill, Pa.

Folsom, Pa.

Linwood, Pa.

Springfield, Pa.

The Gelateria in Primos, Pa.

Theresa and Mike discussing more changes at the Gelateria.

CAN I SHARE SOME THOUGHTS?

Nowhere else on earth could a kid who didn't have a good education grow up and achieve all the things that I've achieved. I love the United States. I love the American flag. I love what it stands for. I love what it allowed me to do. I couldn't have accomplished everything that I have accomplished anywhere else in the world. It just wouldn't have happened anywhere else.

Every building that I own proudly flies the American flag. I watch those flags. I make sure that they are cared for. I make sure that they don't get tattered. I make sure that they are lit. I make sure that they come down before a storm.

The flag watched over me when I was young...I watch over it now. When someone disrespects the flag, it hurts me. It gets me angry. It makes me sad.

Where else could you imagine a young boy, with little education or money growing up, to lead such a wonderful life. Yes, I worked hard, but where else could I have turned $5.00 that my father lent me into over a dozen, solid, real estate investments and more than five active businesses (the numbers change over time: We buy real estate, we sell real estate, we buy businesses, we sell businesses, we get businesses back, we open new businesses, we close some others – luckily, that doesn't happen too often).

People don't realize what a gift it is to live in this country. People don't know what it is like to live under a dictator, or to have your home invaded.

I want others to have the chance that I had to create an incredible life. I want others to respect the flag and the country that I love.

My first visit back to Ellis Island since I came through in 1948.

Ground Zero.

The museum at Ground Zero – a very sobering visit.

My grandson, Matt, and I at Ellis Island with the Freedom Tower in the background.

MY FAMILY – IN THE UNITED STATES

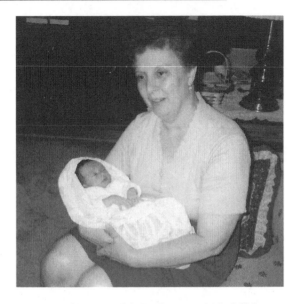

Sara with one of our first grandchildren.

Me with one of our grandchildren.

This was the whole family somewhere around 2000.

My family in the Cocco's Gelateria at 550 Oak Avenue,
Primos – 2015.

Me with my first great-grandchild, Logan – Christmas 2015.

MY FAMILY – IN ITALY

Luigi, me and Massimo in Italy.

Massimo in the Coccos, Primos, Pa. dining room.

Me with Massimo (left). With my daughter, Linda, at Alessio and Emanuela's wedding (right).

Alessio and Emanuela at their wedding.

Massimo (standing) with Butch and Louise Ara.

The family together (including our friends, the Ara's) at Massimo's.

<u>NOTES</u>

p. 119

Made in the USA
Middletown, DE
09 May 2017